GRACE

in

GRIEF

*A 100-Day Journey Exploring God's
Tender Response to Loss*

TINA AKRIDGE

ENDORSEMENTS

This masterpiece is infused with hard-won wisdom, spiritual depth, and healing truth. Tina Akridge has provided a noteworthy tool in how to take unbearable pain and bring understanding to it, as she fosters spiritual growth simultaneously. This great work is purely inspired by the Spirit of the Most High and Holy God and birthed from a journey of devastating loss. Tina Akridge has accomplished something extraordinary in that you will feel deeply understood. You will gain knowledge and wisdom of the Word of God and His incomparable character proven in how He lavishes us with His Love by meeting us precisely where we are. We are complicated by design and hardship intensifies our complexities. Tina Akridge honestly, humbly, and obediently gives her readers an intimate view of her journey through grief. She helps us understand how our design is so intentional by God and is an honest reflection of His image. She describes beautifully how God uses His various names and attributes to meet us where we are, no matter the difficulty we face or the thickness of the darkness. By sharing her own path and lessons learned, she gives us the gift of being met in the ashes and having a companion on the healing journey to beauty and survivorship.

Chana Ashlan Land, M.Ed., LPC, LPCS

Knowing Mark and Tina for many years, walking this journey with them, so many words paint a picture of their lives together with Abba Father by their side. Tina's devotional on God's great grace in the grief of a human soul covers all of her journey as she shares the wisdom Abba Father has given her with every step she has taken. *Grace in Grief* is a raw, real, joyful, heartfelt revelation devotional that can help lead to an inspiring beautiful place in Abba's love and restoration.

Mark Bagwell, President, Shade Tree Ministry

Published by hope*books
2217 Matthews Township Pkwy
Suite D302
Matthews, NC 28105
www.hopebooks.com

hope*books is a division of hope*media

Printed in the United States of America

First paperback edition.

Paperback ISBN: 979-8-89185-082-8
Hardcover ISBN: 979-8-89185-083-5
Ebook ISBN: 979-8-89185-084-2
Library of Congress Number: 2024931113

TABLE OF CONTENTS

Endorsements...ii
Introduction.. 1

I.WHEN WE CAN'T 5
1: When We Can't Breathe 6
2: Blinding Circumstance... 8
3: A Failing Heart.. 10
4: Deaf Ears.. 12
5: Loss of Taste... 14
6: Brain Fog; When We Can't Think, He Clears Our Mind 16
7: No Words.. 18
8: Help My Unbelief.. 20
9: Unforgiveness; He Helps Us Forgive 22
10: Amnesia 24
11: Hope Defined 26
12: Weak in the Knees.. 29
13: Muddling Through 31
14: Empty Cup 33
15: Marred Image.. 35
16: Wonder Restored... 37
17: Advocate 39
18: I Don't Understand 41
19: The Song... 43
20: Stuck 45
21: All Defenses Are Down 47
22: Speechless... 49
23: Unable to Initiate 51
24: No Response 53
25: No Answers... 55

II. WHAT HE DOES 57

26: He Heals Us 58
27: He Redeems Us 60
28: He Calls us 62
29: He Teaches Us 64
30: He Refines Us 66
31: He Forgives Us 68
32: He Unites Us 70
33: He Fights For Us 72
34: He Validates Us 74
35: He Affirms Us 76
36: He Commissions Us 78
37: He Restores Us 80
38: He Hides Us 82
39: He Rescues us 84
40: He Adopts Us 86
41: He Avenges us 88
42: He Cleanses Us 90
43: He Ministers To Us 92
44: He Knows Us 94
45: He Forms Us 96
46: He Settles Us 98
47: He Carries Us 100
48: He Invites Us 102
49: He Creates Us 104
50: He Adorns Us 106

III. WHAT HE SAYS 109

51: "Begin." 110
52: "I've Got This." 112
53: "I'm Not Leaving." 114
54: "I'll Come to You." 116
55: "This Way." 118
56: "You Are Forgiven." 120
57: "I Adore You." 122
58: "I've Got a Good Plan." 124
59: "Worship Me." 126
60: "You Can Trust Me." 128

61: "I AM For You." 130
62: "I Never Sleep." 132
63: "Listen, I am Speaking." 134
64: "I Value You." 136
65: "I'm Near You." 138
66: "Come Take Your Seat." 140
67: "It Is Finished." 142
68: "Do Not Be Afraid." 144
69: "I'm Your Friend." 146
70: "I'm Prepared For This." 148
71: "Ask Me." 150
72: "You are Mine." 152
73: "I'm Getting Things Ready for You." 154
74: "Here I Come, Child!" 156
75: "I Will Make It Right." 158

IV. HOW HE FEELS (ABOUT US) 161
76: He Wants Us 162
77: He is Pleased With Us 164
78: He Chooses Us 166
79: He Connects With Us 168
80: We are the Apple of His Eye 170
81: He Counts the Hairs on Our Head 172
82: He Thinks Highly and Often of Us 174
83: He Values Us 176
84: We're Worth Dying For 178
85: He Loves to Calm Our Fears 180
86: He Sees us as Family 182
87: He Rejoices Over Us! 184
88: God Loves us Steadfastly 186
89: He Feels Generous Towards Us 188
90: He Feels Protective 190
91: He Knows Us By Name 192
92: He feels Mercy Toward Us 194
93: He Feels Abounding in Love 196
94: He is Patient With Us 198
95: He Sees Us As His "Favored" 200
96: He Sees Us Made New 202

97: He Delights in our Praises **204**
98: He Sees Us United with Him **206**
99: He Enjoys Us! **208**
100: He Feels Compassion Towards Us **210**

Acknowledgements: **213**
Meet the Author **214**

INTRODUCTION

Grace in Grief is a transformative journey that delves into the eternal and unconditional love of our Heavenly Father amidst the trials of life. In moments of despair and vulnerability, when we feel breathless, blinded, and unable to cope, God reveals Himself as our Savior, breathing life into us and guiding us through the darkness.

Being married for twenty-five years to an incredible man was the joy of my life. When he was diagnosed with sarcoma, my world became fragile and unsteady. I saw my husband battle hard and cling to his faith. Mark led us well and pointed to Abba Father through all the disappointment, scary treatments, and wobbly faith. He kept his eyes on Christ through all the ripple effects of cancer and loved us so well, even in our disbelief. This leadership brought me from fear to a heart's desire to stand firm in my faith through the fire. I didn't want to miss all God was going to teach me and use me for this season. My goal with this book is to equip you, the reader, to stand after you've done everything else (Ephesians 6:13), strong in your faith and held by our Abba Father, and to assist you to see God right beside you in your hardship, loving you, caring for your needs, and being your Ever Present Help.

This book was conceived in the throes of hardship for me and my family. My husband was a financial advisor who served our community with wisdom, grace, and enthusiasm. When he began his first round of chemotherapy his office manager was overwhelmed with calls from clients wanting updates on how Mark was doing. Mark asked me to start some form of communication that would keep the community abreast of his victories and struggles, making it easier on his office manager. It seemed a little difficult to focus on and maybe even too vulnerable to do, but I agreed.

What I discovered in this practice was that my Lord and Savior was breathing life into me through each journal entry, each post on social

1

media, and each update I penned. As I wrote to inform others, I began to see the hand of God in our circumstances. His care and comfort became so tangible to me. Mark noticed this revived effect writing had on me and immediately began encouraging me to write. "Write a book, Tina. Or just keep doing these updates for others. Your faith comes alive on the pages!" I wrote throughout the eight years we battled cancer. And in his last week, Mark took my hand one day and as my eyes filled with tears, I asked him, "What will I do?" He smiled and said, "Write." I found that in serving others I am filled up to the fullest measure with God, His goodness, His truth, and His hope. My prayer for each of you is that you too will be filled up and satisfied with the love of your Lord and Comforter as you read.

God revives our failing hearts as we trust Him, restoring our wounded souls with His boundless compassion. When we feel lost and unable to hear His voice, God opens our spiritual ears to His gentle whisper, bringing divine understanding. His powerful presence brought me out of the hopelessness of losing Mark after he went to Heaven and surrounded me with truth and strength through His promises. Even when life's hardships leave us unable to taste His goodness, God reminds us of His abundant love, nourishing us with His presence.

Throughout this journey, I learned through His unfailing word that God clears the fog of our minds, providing clarity and wisdom to navigate life's uncertainties. When we can't find words to pray, He intercedes on our behalf, understanding the desires of our hearts. God heals our hearts in moments of doubt and unforgiveness, setting us free with His patient grace.

When our memories fade, and we lose sight of who we are, God reminds us of His faithfulness, writing His truth on the tablet of our hearts. In moments when we feel unable to communicate, our spirits utter noise, and God hears the whispers of our souls, responding with His loving understanding.

God speaks words of comfort, peace, and affirmation through it all. He calls us His beloved children, promising never to leave nor forsake us. In times of turmoil, He invites us to cast our cares upon Him, for He cares for us deeply (1 Peter 5:7). His promises become a soothing balm that comforts our troubled hearts.

God's love for us goes beyond comprehension. He delights in us and sees us as His precious treasures. His patience and boundless love remain unwavering, even when we stumble. God knows us intimately, understanding our thoughts, fears, and desires, even when we can't express them.

As we journey through hardship, may we embrace the unfailing love of our Heavenly Father. I want to walk this journey with you as you seek His peace in your turmoil. His love sustains, guides, and comforts us like an unshakeable anchor in the storms of life. No matter the circumstances, nothing can separate us from the love of God that is in Christ Jesus our Lord.

My hope for you, as you read this book, is that it will be a beacon of truth and solace, reminding you that we are deeply and eternally loved, even in the darkest moments of life. My desire for you is that in these pages, you will find a companion in your faith as you navigate your difficult moments with Abba Father as your guide and Friend. As I have written this devotional, I have paused often, lifted the one who will be reading these words in her darkest night, and asked that The Holy Spirit fill each page, and each heart reading, and be their Great Comforter and Guide.

As we trust in His grace and presence, may we find the strength to grieve, the courage to press on, and the assurance that we are forever held in the arms of our loving Heavenly Father. Please know that you are deeply loved by the One who created you, and He is right beside you, wherever your grief takes you. Let these words and His love heal your wounds and enrich your faith.

I.
WHEN WE CAN'T

There is a kind of hardship that brings us to our knees. It robs us of the normal abilities to reason, process, and make sound decisions. This state of mind also changes our vision of what is truly happening around us and to us. We find ourselves unable to deal with either the daily or unusual things that we face. This section will open our eyes to see our Savior. It will renew our minds with His truth. It will infuse wisdom and strength beyond our personal resources to do for us what we cannot do in these moments. We will see that we have a place to rest and receive from our Heavenly Father as we rely not on our own understanding and abilities but on His strength, wisdom, and power. When we can't, He does for us.

1

WHEN WE CAN'T BREATHE

Sometimes life stops us. We're moving along, and suddenly, we are lifeless. Maybe it's catastrophic, and the wind is instantly knocked out of us. Life calls our bluff, and we're suffocating under its weight. About a year and a half after our first cancer diagnosis in my husband's otherwise healthy body, we got the call. It was back. We had just recovered from the powerful effects of a seven-month cancer regime and enjoyed one and a half years of remission. But with this one phone call, it was all we could do just to stand there, breathless. This kind of news creates internal anxiety. It disconnects us. Steals our ability to engage.

When we face this kind of hardship, we can't even expand our lungs, much less do what is next. But our God is El Roi; The God who *sees* in those moments, hollow and void, unable. And beyond that, He offers to *be* our Breath. Ezekiel 37:3-6 (ESV) shows us God's promise. "Thus says the Lord God to these bones: Behold, I will cause breath to enter you, and you will live." Ezekiel is shown a valley of dry bones. Lifeless bones. Can you relate to looking at your circumstance and feeling like a valley of dry bones? The Lord asks him, "Son of man, can these bones live?" (verse 3). Can they? Can I? Ezekiel simply says, "O Lord God, you know." God breathes life into dry bones. He covers the bones with sinews and flesh (verse 6). As they are reformed, imagine lungs expanding with oxygen as life begins again! What did the bones do to be revitalized? Nothing. The breathless bones did nothing. They couldn't, and nothing was required of them.

My friend, nothing is required of you either. Our very life is from God. He sees us and swoops down into our valley to pour His breath into us. When we are incapable of expanding our lungs to take in the air we so desperately need, He fills our dry bones with His life. And suddenly, we can breathe again! If you find yourself unable to grasp this truth, the Lord, our God declares, "...I have spoken, and I will do it" (verse 14b). Receive His promise of life, and breathe again. And if you can't even do that, just offer up Ezekiel's simple prayer.

"O Lord God, You know."

2

BLINDING CIRCUMSTANCE

There is a point in hardship that is blinding. Sure, we see the physical. We see the items around us. But what we perceive has shifted from truth to uncertainty. We no longer trust the things we once saw clearly. His Ever-Present Help (Psalm 46:1). His promises (Isaiah 41:13). His Companionship (Proverbs 18:24). We can't see Him. We can't see the Truth. This shift of vision comes in the heaviest grief. Under the weight of our sorrow. We see through blurred lenses. We once had tunnel vision when we saw one thing; our profound loss.

As I sat in that Oncology Surgeon's office, the diagnosis choked out my oxygen, future, and hope. My vision had been suddenly altered. All I could see was loss. Cancer. Death. The gifts Abba had lavished on me through a loving husband, beautiful children, a home, and a future all faded into the abyss of this diagnosis. It was all I could see or hear, honestly. This diagnosis made my vision suddenly murky. And with our eyes full of tears, our hearts were just cloudy. We needed help and in that very real moment. We needed something to grab ahold of to get us to the next step. As we took a breath and re-centered ourselves on our all-powerful God, we were able to walk out of that office, get on our knees, and trust Him with this news. When we are willing to surrender the confusion and fear, and simply walk in His promise to hold us, regardless of what we've just heard or even what we see in front of us, we can shift from fear to faith. We can take a breath and take our next step in trusting that Abba will be with us. This changes everything from our nerves to our outlook. Our circumstances don't have to change to exercise our faith.

Still, we weren't sure what to expect. Is help up ahead? Is the proverbial "light at the end of the tunnel" hope or a fast-moving train headed straight for us? We trusted Him, but with every test result, our vision began to get blurred again. One day we just found ourselves squinting with no real insight. Doubting our senses. Questioning what we know. Our truth conflicts with our blurry sight.

Have you ever been there? One phone call and your vision shifts. We stammer through the darkness, wondering who shut off the lights. Who stole our reliable source? Where is our hope? How do we escape this haze that engulfs us?

Friend, Emmanuel is there with us. No condemnation. He sees our lack. He doesn't talk louder, as some do when they see someone blinded. Instead, He offers real help. "I will guide you" (Isaiah 58:11 NIV). He takes our hand and leads us out of the darkness, out of the haze. He gingerly places us in a hiding place where we regain our ability to see the truth. To see Him. And He does it with a steadfast love that we don't always understand. Good news! He doesn't require us to see Him or even understand Him to receive help. Reach up and give Him your hand.

"Father, guide me."

3

A FAILING HEART

If you've walked long enough or through enough on this earth, you can relate to a failing heart. Think of young children. Vibrant. Joyful. Expectant. Their hearts are light and full of hope.

Do you remember when you were a child? As adults, our hearts are still full, but of what? The heaviness that comes with living. We get bogged down with the stuff of life that steals hope from us. Steals our joy. And our hearts fail us.

My husband and I battled cancer for eight and a half years. Through the diagnosis, tests, treatment plans, and results, we slowly got bogged down. Sure, we'd read the promises. He turns our mourning into dancing (Psalm 30:11 ESV). We'd feel renewed, but then more bad news would come our way. More struggle. Eventually, the heaviness took over, and we felt nothing. We flatlined. Can our lifeless hearts be revived?

When our hearts fail, we feel weak. We can't seem to lift our own heads. The Psalmist describes it clearly, "My flesh and my heart fail…" (Psalm 73:26a NKJV). As I read His Word, I feel a surge of energy. The truth is that our hearts do fail. Not just my heart or Mark's, but human hearts. The deeper truth is that God knew this would happen. Romans 15:13 declares the remedy when we find ourselves in this condition. The God of Hope "…fill(s) us with all joy and peace…" as we trust in *Him*. He does this so that we "may overflow with hope…" Not hope we muster up within ourselves from a failed heart. How could we?

It is hope beyond ourselves. "By the power of the Holy Spirit." The rest of Psalm 73:26 proclaims again, "…But God is the strength of my heart." It's not in reading these truths that we are revived. It is in *knowing* them to be true because we *know Him*. He is our source of revival.

When your heart fails, be encouraged. His strength brings us back to life, filling us with hope, joy, and peace. When God gives, it is never just enough. We get supernatural strength accompanied by hope, joy, and peace. And like those children, our hearts become light again.

Your failed heart is no surprise to God. He knows. He sees. He revives. Let Him.

"Father, my heart."

4

DEAF EARS

It's been said, "You have one mouth and two ears. Listen more, talk less." But what happens when we can't hear? We've all lingered in the pool on a hot summer's day and emerged with ears clogged with water. We didn't heed the warning to take a break. And we ended up with deaf ears. This scenario may sound worth it, but regardless of how we get there, hearing impairment frustrates us in any form. It could be physical or spiritual. We can't hear and are robbed of encouragement. Our truth is stolen from us. We get disconnected from God. When life complicates our senses, we struggle to hear the truth. Didn't we heed the warning to slow down? Regroup? Maybe we did, but life just came so fast. Suddenly we were covered up. In those moments, we may think the solution is within ourselves. We tend to lean on checklists and to-dos to resolve problems. If we aren't careful, we can create more hearing loss.

I remember the exhausted awareness that life goes on even in trials. I found myself standing under a mountain of laundry, realizing that despite having just returned from a week-long hospital stay with Mark, my kids had nothing clean to wear to practice. I was determined not to let this laundry mountain be the end of me, so I jumped in. I sorted, washed, dried, folded, and even put away. I was focused for three hours straight. I heard myself saying, "Go, Tina. You've got this! You can do it!" When I came up from that laundry frenzy, I realized I had forgotten to take the kids to their practice! Exhausted, I lay on my bed and thought, "I can't do this, Lord. I'm too tired."

When we aren't able to hear, it affects our equilibrium, and we lose our balance and our direction. Haven't we always tried to fix ourselves? We can't see, so we put on glasses. In the same way, we need to look at what lens, or what perspective, we are seeing our circumstances through. Are we looking at our circumstances through the lens of truth? God's truth or our own? When we don't understand something, we turn to ourselves and attempt a self-reliant strength. We rely on our finite minds. How does that work for us? Honestly, it creates more questions. As a child, I'd eventually have to humbly ask for help unclogging stuffy swimmers' ears. A few drops of alcohol and vinegar, and I could hear again.

When chaos deafens us, we can try our own healing methods or go to The Healer. Philippians 4:19 reminds us through Christ, "My God will supply every need of yours, according to His riches of His glory in Christ Jesus." In Christ, all our needs are met. Let's let Him hold us in His hands, and as He did in Mark 7:34, command our ears to "Be opened." He alone can do this. He wants us to come to Him. Have you found yourself with deaf ears? Ask the Healer. He is able. He is willing. Receive.

"Lord, open my ears."

5

LOSS OF TASTE

Covid introduced a new symptom to our bodies. Loss of smell and taste. The two are interwoven. Smell entices our taste buds, enhancing our taste. When our ability to smell is gone, our taste dissipates. Have you experienced this loss of taste? Covid visited our home as well. And I found that this loss of smell and taste also affected my desire to eat. Without the ability to smell or taste, my appetite diminished. The whiff of spicy chili or creamy risotto couldn't arouse my appetite. I forgot what things tasted like. I had to hold up a strawberry and set my mind to intentionally focus on what a strawberry tastes like. Sweet. Juicy. Like summer. I had to exert more energy into the act of eating without my sense of taste. I ate anyway. Our bodies need fuel. Yet, I had no enjoyment. No desire.

Like COVID-19, life can steal our taste and appetite. When we no longer taste, we forget what is *good*. Scripture invites us to "Taste and see that the Lord is good!" (Psalm 34:8 NIV). Why? Why can't we just read or hear it? Why does the Psalmist use this sense to describe God's goodness? We can mechanically lift our forks without our sense of taste. Fill our mouths. Chew. Swallow. The act of feeding our body is accomplished. But the invitation to taste is to *enjoy*!

Tasting and seeing that God is good fills our spirits with delicious nourishment. It takes us beyond just reading, speaking, or hearing. It allows us to *enter in*. We're not just fed, we're *satisfied*. Delighted. Engaged. Our soul craves more than just fuel. It hungers for Delight. Relationship. Satisfaction. Intentionally soaking up His Word provides sustenance that meets our longings and moves us from methodical living to a *satisfied* life. God desires us to *enjoy* Him. Have you lost your sense of taste? Enter in. Linger in His Word. Allow yourself five minutes or two hours, whatever you can mentally afford, and just sit in His Word. I have found the practice of reading a verse or two and journaling about it helps me to experience His truth on a deeper level. It resets my heart and allows me to receive His good. The key here is grace. Give yourself the grace to read one verse or one chapter. It's okay to sit and linger or grab and go. However long you can linger, you won't be disappointed.

"Father, I will taste and see."

6

BRAIN FOG; WHEN WE CAN'T THINK, HE CLEARS OUR MIND

Brain fog can result from so many things. Lack of sleep, grief, stress, or just too much going on at once. Regardless of the source, it can be frustrating. Did you know? God has a remedy. The Prince of Peace has a promise for us. "You keep him in perfect peace whose mind is stayed on you, because he trusts in you" (Isaiah 26:3). So, how are we kept in this perfect peace? Trust Him. Sometimes life gets so complicated and heavy. We can't seem to think clearly. Grief has a way of covering us in a shroud of darkness. Everything seems too hard or too confusing. We can't seem to think our way out of the hole our grief has created. In these times, even our minds fail us. God knows this. He has simplified His help for us. Trust Him.

We can open His word, soak in it, and meditate on it.

I am also familiar with a kind of grief that robs a person of the ability to meditate or to be steadfast about anything. After Mark died, it seemed a floodgate gushed open, demanding I make so many decisions immediately. I found myself frozen in fear and overwhelmed with emotions. I couldn't think straight. I doubted my own ability to make a clear decision because I felt muddled and uncertain and, frankly, alone. The enemy would have us rot there in that isolation. But there's more. "The unfolding of your words gives light; it imparts understanding to the simple" (Psalm 119:130 ESV). We don't have to be some scholar who can dissect and dig deep into a theological dialogue. Our mind does not have to be sharp and alert to pick up our Bible.

Open it. Unfold His word. Lift your eyes to the page, and receive. "Draw near to God and He will draw near to you" (James 4:8a). As I bowed my head and took first my weary heart, and then each decision quietly before my Lord, He calmed my heart and settled my mind.

He promises to go the extra mile when all we can do is show up. All we have to do is open our eyes. Turn towards Him. He will clear your mind and refresh your soul. Time in His presence cleans our hearts and clears our minds. It's one of the benefits of being with Him. The Psalmist tells us, "The law of the Lord is perfect, refreshing the soul" (Ps.19:7 NIV). To refresh is to give new strength, to restore (Merriam-Webster. com). In His Presence, through opening His Word, He steps into our foggy brains and pours out refreshment. Let Him bring clarity to your weary mind today.

"Help me to unfold Your Holy word today."

7

NO WORDS

The phone slips from your hands onto the floor. Your body stiffens, your knees lock, and your arms go limp. The room goes dark. You can't seem to catch your breath. A bad report from the doctor, and the other proverbial shoe drops. In these times, words escape us. Our mind seems to stop at the end of that dreaded sentence just spoken into our soul. We want to cry out, shake our fists, or beg for help. Instead, we're silent. We're stuck in this inability to formulate a prayer.

We were six years into our battle with cancer when our oldest came to us and said, "I need help." He then shared that he had been drinking nonstop and needed help to get out of his situation. My mind almost burst, trying to grasp the struggle he had kept to himself as we were wrestling with Mark's battle. I wanted to scream, but at whom? Him? Myself? God? I wanted to pray, but I had no words. Unable to communicate what my soul longs to bellow out. And I remain silent, yet restless.

The silence is deafening, yet no words will come. What do we do when we can't pray? Romans 8:26 (NIV) covers this desperate need within. "In the same way, the Spirit helps us in our weakness." He knows where we are in these moments when we feel invisible. Helpless. Unable to move. "...The Spirit Himself intercedes for us through wordless groans." Some translations say "...with groanings too deep for words." In my groaning over Mark and my son, I felt His Spirit come from within and lift my ache for my family. He intercedes when I have no words.

When you suddenly lose yourself and are sure no one is around, He is there. With you. No words are needed. He knows exactly what your soul lacks. He steps into your profound grief and speaks on your behalf to Abba Father. They communicate so intimately that no human words need be formed. What's more, Jesus intercedes on our behalf. Always. Scripture tells us He is "at the right hand of God, who indeed is interceding for us" (Romans 8:34). Again, in Hebrews 7:25b, Paul reminds us that Christ "lives to make intercession for (us)."

Not only does His Holy Spirit intimately communicate to the Father when we are frozen in our grief or trial, but Jesus, our Savior, lives to intercede on our behalf. He's got us covered. When we can't pray, He prays for us. When we can't speak, rest in who He is, our Intercessor.

"Jesus."

8

HELP MY UNBELIEF

There's a kind of hardship that grips us. It stops us in our tracks and tries to erase the truth we know. It changes us. We go from trust to distrust. From walking with our hand in His to listless arms dangling empty. And God is aware. He sees our deepest needs, our darkest thoughts, and our faithless hearts. And He calls us. He brings assistance in our unbelief. Jeremiah 3 meets Israel in a similar, dark, faithless place. God calls out to His own, yet they ignore him. They continue in their disobedience. And He extends grace and healing.

After eight years of battling my husband's cancer, I was in a dark place. A place of lifelessness. A temptation to indulge in disbelief that God would allow or tolerate such a ravenous disease to course through a man's body. A man surrendered to his Lord and Savior. I found myself wrestling with faithlessness. And God met me there.

When we find ourselves struggling with Truth, it's a good time to look up. He does not hide from us in those times. He isn't shocked by our frail humanity. He knows all about us. He saw every day of ours at the beginning of all time. Before the foundations of the world were laid. (Psalm 139) We don't surprise Him with unbelief. He sees, and He calls to us. He invites us to come to Him with our doubt and surrender it to Him. It doesn't surprise or even offend Him. He can handle our uncertainty and questions in times of doubt. In the middle of chaos and sin, He extends His forgiveness to Israel. "Return...I will heal your faithlessness" (Jeremiah 3:22).

When we come to the end of ourselves and our faith, Abba Father extends healing and restoration. His heart is Love. He knows our fragile hearts and provides what we cannot provide for ourselves. Hope.

Forgiveness. Healing. When you find yourself in unbelief, take heart. He is there with you. As the father in Mark 9:24 admits, "I believe. Help my unbelief!" God heard this honest prayer. He will hear yours too. And He will extend healing and hope in your time of unbelief.

"Lord, help my unbelief."

9

UNFORGIVENESS; HE HELPS US FORGIVE

Have you ever felt like you just can't forgive someone? Ever crashed into a wall of inability? No access to the place in your heart where forgiveness comes in and allows you to move forward? You've tried, but it keeps coming back up, and you're just stuck in unforgiveness. So, then what?

In my grief, I found a vulnerability in my heart towards unforgiveness. My loss created a perfect environment to harbor hurt. I found when someone would say something harmful, or act unkindly towards me as I mourned, it was almost second nature to hold onto that hurt, push it down, and think, "I'll address that later when I have more mental energy to deal with it." The calloused doctor who spoke harshly about Mark's diagnosis. The flippant nurse who thought we were being too sensitive. The neighbors who spoke harshly to my kids because they thought my kids weren't thankful enough for the dinner. I was using every ounce of mental and emotional energy I had just to make it through the next moment. Sometimes I was being "too sensitive," and other times people were just being cruel. All of this created an environment to harbor hurt and push the command to forgive onto the back burner while we got through another day. Yet, when we brush off the need to forgive someone, something begins to fester within us. God loves us too much to let that go unattended. Even in our grief, forgiveness is crucial for our spiritual health.

Understanding forgiveness will help us take the first step toward forgiving someone else. Forgiveness is bringing a hurt, or sin, to God and asking for the blood of Jesus to remove it. Forgiveness is not between you and the offender. It's between you and God. He knows that unforgiveness breeds malice and anger, hatred and hostility. Those things keep us from receiving forgiveness and grace ourselves. So, God, in His mercy, commands us to forgive as He has forgiven us.

My grandmother's last words to me were, "Forgive. Forgive. Forgive." She knew of some unforgiveness I had been harboring. She saw it growing slowly and changing my attitude as well as outlook. In my unforgiveness, I was allowing bitterness and resentment to intrude into my heart, mind, and attitude towards a family member. She saw it change me. She died at the ripe age of 84 years old and had lived with unforgiveness. She had tasted the bitter fruit it produced. She had surrendered her hurt to Abba Father and knew it was worth letting go and trusting God. She wanted that for me too.

God doesn't take unforgiveness lightly. It's not some watery suggestion God gestures towards us flippantly. Seeing forgiveness as a command helps get our attention to its importance. If we think about the Father's heart, we must ask why He commands it? Matthew 6:14-15 tells us that if we don't forgive others' sins against us, God will not forgive our sins. How can God ask so much of us? Because His Son came to die and forgive us. "...while we were still sinners, Christ died for us" (Romans 5:8). He is just. He made a way, the only way, for us to be forgiven. We cannot save ourselves or pay the high price required to forgive sin. Yet, in unforgiveness, we are withholding Christ's sacrifice extended to all. A just God cannot allow this. He sent His Son to cover the cost so we could be forgiven. Because Christ died to forgive man of sin, we must also forgive. He gives us this promise to hold fast to in 1 John 1:9 (NIV): "If we confess our sins, he is faithful and just, and will forgive us our sins and purify us from all unrighteousness." We have this promise that He will forgive us.

As we experience His forgiveness, we find the strength to extend forgiveness to others. As we ponder what forgiveness is and how God has lavishly extended it to us, He can work a miracle in us to do what we can't do on our own: forgive. Give Him your heavy heart and the wounds of unforgiveness, and let His Son's blood wipe away the stains of sin, both yours and others who have sinned against you. And be set free.

"Lord, please help me to forgive as You have forgiven me."

10

AMNESIA

In deep sorrow, we can forget things. We forget details, dates, times, and other key pieces of a specific event. This can happen during a traumatic experience. It can also become a way of living. We get caught up in this life, and we forget. Losing our memory can result in losing other things. The struggle we endured as we walked through this cancer battle clouded my image of the God I know and trust. I found myself shut up in my sunroom. I was reading His word and listening to praise music but had not invited God in. Fear and anxiety had become my closest friends. I began to see myself as a hopeless child of God, crippled with fear and doubt. My identity became my battle instead of a child of the King of kings. Lost in a false identity, I was losing heart and faith.

In Deuteronomy 4, the Israelites lost their identity. They forgot who they were and whose they were. Their amnesia affected their behavior and attitude. And they sinned against their God. Sometimes, in losing our memory of who we are, we, too, sin. And our memory can be stripped of God's promise. But God, in Deuteronomy 4:31, declares His character and reminds them, and us, of His promise. "For the Lord, your God is a merciful God. He will not leave you or destroy you or forget the covenant with your fathers that He swore to you." This promise is rich in showing us the heart of our God. His promises are not dependent on our behavior, attitude, or memory. He reminds us that He will do what He says, independent of us, our actions, or our memory.

We can also lose our purpose in life." Exodus 9:16 states our purpose clearly. "For this purpose, I have raised you up, to show my power, so that my name may be proclaimed in all the earth." When we hold fast to our faith in the middle of our hardship, others around us are pointed to the Savior of all mankind. They are reminded that, like us, God is there for them in their struggle. We get an audience to proclaim His power and goodness to anyone who will listen. Not only does He remind us of who we are and our purpose, but He swoops down and offers help. "I cry out to God most high, to God who fulfills his purpose for me" (Psalm 57:2). He fulfills our purpose.

When we can't remember the truth, God reminds us who He is through His Word. He reminds us who we are too. In His loving-kindness and steadfast love, He reminds us that we are His, and He is good and in control. Rest in this truth, and know He never forgets us.

"Lord, remind me."

HOPE DEFINED

Hope. What do you think of when you hear that word? Oxford Language defines it as "a feeling of expectation and desire for a certain thing to happen." Merriam-Webster defines hope as "...to want something to be true."(Merriam-Webster.com) Our world today is desperate for hope, especially since the pandemic. But if hope is defined as merely a feeling or a desire, it's empty. Yet, we know from reading His Word, God tells us to hope.

If God puts such emphasis on hope, it isn't empty. Maybe our definition needs to be stronger. The Hebrew word for hope is qawa (verb) and tiqwa (noun), "to trust and wait expectantly." (Biblestudytools. com) If God is telling us to wait and expect, we know that what He is telling us to hope for will come to pass. That definition is meatier. That's something we can hold onto. So, what should we hope for? And what should we expect? Let's look at His Word.

It's one thing to have the proper definition of hope, and the second piece to this weightier hope is to know what to put our hope in. We see in Jeremiah 29:11(NIV) that it's God who gives us our hope. "For I know the plans I have for you," declares the Lord, "plans to prosper you and not harm you, plans to give you hope and a future." He gives us hope in His faithful promise to guide us in this life. He has it all planned out. He's Sovereign, and His plans are for our good. This charge to hope remains true even when things don't turn out the way we thought they would. Mark and I had good plans to share out of the generosity and kindness God had shown to us. We would love our neighbors, friends, enemies, and community and share God's love with whomever He brought into our lives. We would stand firm in our faith in Him and be the light in this dark world. That was our plan, to shine and further the kingdom through living our faith out loud together.

That was a good plan, but not God's good plan for us, as He promised He was carrying out for both Mark and me. So after saying goodbye to the love of my life, my partner on this earth, to spread the Gospel and do good, I was left with a decision to make; to trust God still to carry out this good plan in my life, or to close up shop, and remain lost in my grief and unbelief. When life turns out different from what we planned, we all have that same decision to make. God knew we would face this kind of loss and disappointment. So, He called us to hope. Hope in Him. With all the power, authority, and desire to carry out His promises to us, He asks us to hope, even when it's hard to understand. Our God is the God of hope. We can trust that He will not go against His word. And not only that. Do you see what else comes with hope in God? Joy and peace.

After Mark's death, I was initially heavy with a hopeless feeling. I had prayed for my will to be done, for Mark to wake up with new lungs, and for all cancer to leave his body. But God, in His kindness, gave Mark what was best. That was hard to wrap my brain around as I sat in an empty house without my loved one. Yet, I knew that I didn't know better than God. I knew I couldn't possibly fully understand His ways. Nor was I qualified to determine what "good" truly was. With a finite mind, we humans can't know what is the best outcome. But we can trust that He does. Meditating on this truth as I surrendered my hurt, loneliness, and great loss to Him ushered in His peace and, yes, joy in trusting Him.

We gain joy and peace as we rely on His Word and trust that He will do what He says. And our hope overflows by the power of the Holy Spirit. Isaiah says, "Those who hope in the Lord will renew their strength. They will soar on wings like eagles; they will run and not grow weary; they will walk and not be faint." Hope in our Lord renews and strengthens us. We gain a second wind. Now, who couldn't use a second wind?

I need to point out that this is not just wishful thinking. This is trusting that the Almighty will deliver on all of His promises. This is waiting as we struggle through this life, expecting that He will be our guide, rescue, and salvation. In the here and now, and when He comes to take us to be with Him in Heaven. This is an action. We engage our faith as we set our hope on Him. We can see through His Word that hope is from God and that it's a necessary thing to have and do.

When we hope, wait in expectation, in God's promises, our souls are refreshed, our spirits are encouraged, and our future is secure. Jesus is our hope! As we focus on the One who tells us to hope in Him and trust His promises, hope becomes a blessed assurance to our hearts, minds, and souls. That is what this world needs today. That is what we have in God; His hope. Let's allow ourselves to hope in Him today.

"Lord, my hope is in You."

12

WEAK IN THE KNEES

When we get weak in the knees because of the weight of this world, it can seem we are alone. It can seem that even God has hidden Himself from us. Yet, time and again, He tells us the truth about where He is when we are in the throes of hardship. Deuteronomy 1:31 (NIV) clearly shows our Father God's heart toward us: "There you saw how the Lord your God carried you, as a father carries his son, all the way you went until you reached this place." The Hebrew word for grace is an action of stooping down, or "to stoop down in kindness to another as a superior to an inferior" (Strongs 2603).

Have you ever seen a daddy do this? A child tugs at Daddy's pant sleeve, unable to walk one more step. He stoops down, scoops his child up, and carries them. That is grace. That is what Abba Father does for us. "He tends his flock like a shepherd; He gathers the lambs in his arms and carries them close to His heart" (Isaiah 40:11a).

There were many times I would be drudging through this hardship of Mark battling cancer, watching him lose energy and limbs, and feeling as though I could not take one more step. In total exhaustion, I would plop down on my knees and cry out, "Abba! I can't." Each time He met me with a grace that engulfed me. He scooped me up with open arms, held me close, and whispered His truth and promises into my hurting soul. He is so faithful. It's critical to see the Father's Heart of God with this perspective. Abba Father doesn't snatch us up, disgusted with our lack of strength. He doesn't roll His eyes at us with an unwilling heart. The God of the universe stoops down, cups us in His arms, and holds us near to His heart.

Let this truth penetrate your mind and bring peace to your spirit.

When life overwhelms you, pause, and take a moment to assess your state of mind. I have found that taking slow, intentional breaths calms my mind and body. I think more clearly and can refocus my thoughts on God. When we give ourselves this pause, we can better think about what we need at the moment. A shout-out to a friend, just asking for them to pray for you, does wonders. Maybe you can call someone you trust and ask them to pray at that moment for you or read a verse to help you penetrate your mind with His peace. Sometimes just changing your scenery and stepping outside to face the sun or soak up some raindrops can recenter us into His truth. You will be surprised how a simple act like one of these will lift your spirits and encourage your soul.

We see how God feels what we feel in Isaiah 63:9 (NIV), "In all their distress, he too was distressed, and the angel of his presence saved them. In his love and mercy, he redeemed them; he lifted them up and carried them." Let yourself ponder this beautiful truth. His heart is for us, Friend. His desire and determination are to carry His own and to be the source we press into when we can't take another step. When things get too heavy. When circumstances throw us from our sure footing. A diagnosis. A divorce. A death. A global pandemic. We can't find strength on our own to get back up. Rest in the truth that He is our firm foundation. He swoops down with His Father's heart and carries us when we are weak in the knees.

"Father, carry me."

13

MUDDLING THROUGH

Ever find yourself muddling through your day? I have been there. Things get so heavy it can feel like events, emotions, and duties are pushing you. With listless hearts, we get up, do, and get buried in the weight of the burdens of our lives. Did you know you have a Helper who will carry those burdens with you? "Blessed be the Lord, who daily bears us up; God is our salvation" (Psalm 68:19). Sounds good, but what does this look like? First, we need to humble ourselves. That feeling that you can't carry all of this on your own is true. We weren't made to. But His word guides us through the steps to surrendering all our burdens to our Savior. And it comes with a promise. "Cast your burdens on the Lord, and he will sustain you; he will never permit the righteous to be moved" (Psalm 55.22). He won't let us be moved. Taking time intentionally on these days to meditate on who God is, all of Him, or at least as much as we can comprehend, will allow your muddled mind to refocus. Refocus on Him. That's what true humility does for us. It lets us see who He really is, and who we really are as well. We are a created creature dependent on Him, for every breath, every good thing, our strength, wisdom, and all the fruits of the Spirit, too. On muddled days, these truths will help. In this cleared space, lay each burden down at Almighty's feet.

You know, the move that breaks us in half and drowns us. Defeated, depleted, and surrounded by unattended relationships. We could go there, broken and drowning, unable to do the daily work of life. We all know what that does for our schedules, families, and relationships. It crushes them and us. But He promises that He will carry our burdens with us, lighten our load, and strengthen us with His truth. "Come to me, all who are labor and are heavy laden, and I will give you rest. Take my yoke upon you, and learn from me, for I am gentle and lowly in heart, and you will find rest for your souls. For my yoke is easy, and my burden is light" (Matthew 11:28-30). See how Christ describes Himself? Gentle and lowly. Approachable.

After we humble ourselves and admit we need help, simply go to Him. This can look however you need it to. First thing in the morning, before the rest of the house starts stirring. Mid-afternoon, when the little ones lay down for a nap. At day's end, when the house gets quiet again. It can even be when you're waiting in the pick-up line at school. Quiet the music, close your eyes, and be with Abba Father. Cast your cares on Him. All of them. The ones that are blinding you and the annoying ones that distract you. He cares about them all. Not only does He care, but He also wants to lighten your load.

When He does this, we can take a full breath again. This lets us see this life as the gift it is. Not a muddled-through burden. A gift from your Heavenly Father, who made you from the beginning. His treasure. Valued by Him. His image-bearer. When you find yourself muddled down, humble yourself. Go to your Abba Father. And let Him lighten your load and change your outlook on your life. He can handle it all.

"Father, please take this."

14

EMPTY CUP

Picture this. School has started. Schedules are in full swing. It's a race from the morning alarm to rushing into bed at day's end. Sleeping fast to stay ahead of the next day. Breakfast, rushing to school and work. Practices for extracurricular activities. Returning home to eat, tackling homework, and jumping into bed. This is how most of us live. It can drain our minds, hearts, and souls. We go, go, go until we are empty. Can anyone relate?

None of these things are wrong or bad for us. Yet, we can quickly run out of gas when we are always on the go. Or worse, run out of grace, patience, and love for those around us. And if you throw into the mix a major hardship, your resources are depleted before you even begin sometimes. Understandable. Yet, we can't live out the fruits of the Spirit when we are empty. Being patient, or even kind is a real battle when we have nothing to give. So what can we do? We can receive.

The Psalmist could relate to this fast-paced, emptying lifestyle. He didn't have soccer practice or homework, but he ran on his own strength until it ran out. He found himself needing to receive from God, too. Where did David find his fill-up? "You make known to me the path of life; you will fill me with joy in your presence, with eternal pleasures at your right hand" (Psalm 16:11 NIV). David went to God. He got into His presence and received. We see this available strength again in John 10:10 (NIV). We know the enemy loves to distract us and drain us of strength and hope. Jesus gives the solution, "The thief comes to steal, kill, and destroy; I have come that they may have life and have it to the full."

Jesus does not take and drain. Neither does He expect us to muster the strength to handle this life, much less shine for Him, within our own strength. He never intended for us to use or even have the strength on our own. He empowers us. He fills us to the top with His life, His strength. He is all we need. When we receive from Jesus, we lack nothing. The next time you feel empty, quiet your soul, look to your Savior, and receive Him.

"Jesus, I receive."

15

MARRED IMAGE

Marred is defined as impairing or disfiguring the image of something. (Oxford Languages) There is a kind of heaviness that can disfigure our view of who we are and why we are on this earth. Our image of who we are can get skewed. We begin to see the world, ourselves, or our purpose distortedly. When this happens, our image-bearing becomes marred too.

The hurt we experience through hardship can muddy how we reflect His image. This can rob our eyes of the light to see the truth. We need help to clear out the hurt to properly reflect His image again. I remember the first time (of many) when I fell prey to this. I was tired, scared, and had no real answers for anyone. I was in line to pick up a prescription for my husband for nausea as he waited, sick, in the car. I felt my blood start to boil as they delayed my order for almost an hour. I was done with waiting. I was done with any patience I had walked into the store with, and I was about to lose it. I went to check on him in the car. He was weak but could see my agitation. He touched my arm as I turned to go back in and fight whoever got in my way of getting his medicine, and said, "Tina, remember Whose you are in there. Ok?" His words of truth melted my heart.

Mark was right to lead me to God's truth and His ways at that moment. I prayed a prayer of both forgiveness and a plea for help beyond myself to be the light. This simple prayer and honest moment of surrender helped me to trust His care for us. And I am not alone in this need for God's help in our hearts. David turns his gaze to God's Word to clear his marred vision. His choice to meditate on the Word of God kept his heart likened to His Father's, and acted as a safety guard against growing bitter and distant from God. "The law of the Lord is perfect, refreshing the soul. The statutes of the Lord are trustworthy, making wise the simple. The precepts of the Lord are right, giving joy to the heart. The commands of the Lord are radiant, giving light to the eyes. The fear of the Lord is pure, enduring forever. The decrees of the Lord are firm, and all of them are righteous" (Psalm 19:7-11 NIV). In His word, we gain proper eyesight, wisdom, joy, refreshment, endurance, and a right view of Him. When we turn inward, thinking only of our hurts and needs, this repositions us into a place of self. We forget that our God shall supply all our needs according to His riches in glory (Philippians 4:19 NIV). We become the ones desiring to be served instead of, like Christ, who being the very nature of God, took the position of a servant (Philippians 2:7 NIV). This robs us of our image-bearing calling.

Our needs are valid. God says He will meet all of them. As we press into this truth and trust Him to keep His word and care for us, we are free to love as He loves. This properly reflects the image of our Creator God. Only when we press in, lay our needs at His feet, and trust Him can we love sincerely. With a renewed view of who we are, Whose we are, and why we are here, we can find fulfillment in knowing Abba has our every need met. In this truth, we are free to serve, give, and live the way He created us to live. Will you trust Him to meet your needs, so you can properly reflect His image?

"Jesus, correct my view."

16

WONDER RESTORED

Defined as a feeling of surprise mingled with admiration caused by something beautiful and inexplicable (Oxford Languages), *wonder* brings excitement and hope into our lives. We need daily doses of amazement and inexplicable beauty to give us a bigger picture of our world and our circumstances. Wonder moves us to worship the One who made all of life. The One who saved our soul.

What happens when we lose our wonder? Sometimes we get bogged down with the stuff of life. Our hearts get heavy and cluttered. The weight of this life seems to crush our hope. It's not something we willingly admit, but we've all experienced a lack of wonder. How do we get it back? Psalm 33:8 says, "Let all the earth fear the Lord, let all the inhabitants of the world stand in awe of Him!"

To regain our wonder, we need only to stand in awe. To look at His creation, the intricate details of a flower, the laser focus of an ant, the face of a child holding a blade of grass. Every day, take one minute and look at God's world. Allow yourself to stop and stare for just one minute. When we are in grief, this seems harder to do than at other times in our lives. Yet, quieting our minds and hearts and focusing instead on God's wonder can give us a renewed spirit and allow us to see His goodness, even in hardship. It may take more intention, but take a minute and look outside. Watch your heart fill with awe at His goodness and creativity.

Even as I write this, a steady rain surprises me and saturates the parking lot, refreshing the plants and cleaning the dirt off the cars. I have a choice. Continue in my groove, writing furiously to reach my quota, heavy with the burden that awaits me the moment I focus back on my schedule or my hard situation. Or sit back, watch the drops drip down the palm tree, and let myself be in wonder of a Father who cares for the plants and birds with His generous and timely rain. I choose to be in awe. My mind is refreshed as I soak in His wonder.

Your stuff might still be there, weighing heavy on your heart, but this practice of standing in awe shifts your thinking from the burden to your God. Luke 5:26 says, "And amazement seized them all, and they glorified God and were filled with awe, saying 'We have seen extraordinary things today.'" God created us to worship when we experience awe. It fuels our hearts and sets our spirits in alignment with our Father. We remember His power, involvement, and promises.

The next time you feel void of wonder, take an intentional moment. Go outside. Look around. Let yourself be in awe and worship the God of the universe and your heart. Exodus 15:11 says, "Who is like you, O Lord, among the gods? Who is like you, majestic in holiness, awesome in glorious deeds, doing wonders?" If we allow it, we will see His wonder everywhere. If we take it in, we will experience the hope and excitement that wonder brings into our lives. Today, Pause. Soak it in. And be amazed.

"Father, help me see your wonder today."

17

ADVOCATE

An advocate is someone who speaks on behalf of someone else. Advocates are necessary to help someone feel supported and heard. Have you ever fallen on your knees before the Father only to lose all your words? Your mind is racing, screaming even. Your heart is swollen with fear, sorrow, and confusion. Yet, as you kneel to pray, no words come. And you can't seem to communicate your greatest need at the moment. Oh, I have been there, my friend. I have been so struck with fear or anxiety that I can't even bow my knee, much less utter one single word. I have stood frozen in fear and trembling as we faced another bad test result with uncertainty and frailty. And yet, God was there. He saw my family so hurt we had no words.

I have some comforting news for you. There is one who advocates for us. He stands in our place and represents us. Expresses the heaviness and ache of our souls. Completing His ministry on this earth, as Jesus was about to leave this world and return to heaven, He encouraged the hearts of His disciples with this promise, "And I will ask the Father, and he will give you another advocate to help you and be with you forever" (John 14:16 NIV). Forever we have one who will stand in our place, represent us, and plead our case.

This advocate is the most qualified to represent us. He chose to come to this earth, wrap Himself in flesh, die, and rise again for us. He is familiar with all the things we face as humans. The things that bring us to our knees. He is no stranger to the grief and sorrow of this life that takes our words away. It could be sheer grief or honest sin that robs us of our ability to speak. We feel exhausted or unworthy. And we cannot communicate what our hearts ache for. But there is one who can. Hebrews 8:1-2 (NIV) validates the worthiness of our Advocate. "...

We do have such a high priest, who sat down at the right hand of the throne of the Majesty in heaven, and who serves in the sanctuary, the true tabernacle set up by the Lord, not a mere human."

Not only is He familiar with the hardship of this world, but His rightful place is on the throne. He knows our anguish, loves us purely and completely, and can plead our case. He steps in and covers us with His grace as He speaks to the Father on our behalf, and we are heard. Do we deserve this representation? No. But it's not about us. It's about the Savior of this world and the lover of our soul. The One who took our place continues to do so until He returns to bring us Home. He is our Savior. Our Creator. Our Advocate. When life chokes the words out of us, and we cannot represent ourselves, let's rest in the assurance of our Great Advocate.

"Jesus, represent me."

18

I DON'T UNDERSTAND

There are times when our human minds get blown. What we see and what we know gets discombobulated. Our understanding fails. It throws us into a vain attempt to explain what's happening. We get angry. We feel desperate. We search with our human minds for human explanations. We seek man's ideas when our own fail.

Before we even began to battle, the diagnosis alone caused me to be frantic, with no understanding of what was happening or coming next. My mind just could not comprehend all of it. I needed answers or at least direction. Abba was prepared. Every human mind comes to the end of its ability. God knew this would happen. So he tucked this sage advice into the book of wisdom: "Trust the Lord with all your heart, and do not lean on your own understanding. In all your ways submit to him, and he will make your paths straight" (Proverbs 3:5-6 NIV). This version depicts the cure for getting all tied up in human thinking, relying on a flawed human mind. It says, "Submit to him." This positions us in humility to acknowledge that we don't know. We can't figure it out. It frees us from running in circles, chasing the illusion of our human understanding.

Sometimes we don't get it. The Father knew we would come to the end of ourselves. He meets us there with a promise. He will make our paths straight. He will clear the way and show us the next move. He will give us what we need at the exact moment. This is difficult. It requires trust. And He is trustworthy. Whether you fully comprehend or not. He is faithful. His ways are best. He invites us into this space where we do not have to save ourselves. In Isaiah 1:18-19, He opens His arms of love, extending grace, forgiveness, and a way forward: "Come now, let us reason together; though your sins are like scarlet, they shall be as white as snow; though they are red like crimson, they shall become like wool."

He knows our sin, our lack, our inability to understand. Yet, he calls us to come. Just come. And He will take care of the rest. It does come with a required attitude. "If you are willing and obedient, you shall eat the good of the land…" (vs.19).

Humans don't like not knowing. We don't want to admit when we don't understand. I know that wrestling with no answers and so many fears and concerns makes us anxious. But there is healing and growth that takes place when we lay all our concerns, fears, and emotions at His feet and trust. As usual, we get more than we ever let go of. It's not a fair trade, but it always weighs in our favor. Proverbs 14:12 warns, "There is a way that seems right to a man, but its end is the way to death." We can't understand, and He doesn't require that of us. He offers a clear, right path with a lavish supply of what we need. What we can do is be willing and obedient. The next time you find yourself not understanding, surrender. Obey. And let Abba Father lead.

"Lord, I will rely on You."

19

THE SONG

My mother was a singer. She sang beautifully. She sang in public and in the shower. She sang in the car, the kitchen, and the yard. She always had a song on her lips. She was a woman described as a lover. She loved people well. She by no means had a happy life. She struggled for decades with the sins of others that affected her. Yet, she sang. She chose joy. Everyday.

There is a scripture I love to meditate on: Zephaniah 3:17. It's nestled right smack in the middle of turmoil and disobedience. Right where you'd expect it, right? The Israelites were turning away from their only Savior. Their Creator. Their God. God judged Israel's enemies. Then he judged the nation of Israel. And then we read, "The Lord your God is in your midst, a mighty one who will save; he will rejoice over you with gladness; he will quiet you with his love; he will exult over you with loud singing." This seems out of place. He judges them one minute and sings the next. Have you ever wondered why? God can see all things at all times. He is not bound by time as we are. He knows all. Sees all. And is in control of all.

In this seemingly misplaced scripture, Abba Father sees a time when his people are free from sin and the snares of the flesh. He knows that a time will come when He saves us once and for all from this sin-sick world. When that day comes, we will stand side by side with Him. The walk that started in the Garden of Eden will resume in Heaven. All of heaven rejoices when one sinner is saved. Imagine when we all stand face to face with the Creator and Savior of all mankind. There will be rejoicing. There will be singing.

My mom rested in this truth. She knew that one day, God would wipe away every sin and the effects of sin and set her free. She chose to live in that truth even before she saw it come to pass. We have that choice too. So today, if you feel you've disappointed God, know He sees us for what He will bring us to that day.

Maybe today you feel injured by the sins of others. He understands that fully well. He is familiar with our sins and our sorrows. And He sings over us and quiets us with his love. Not because we are doing it right and deserve it, but because it is His will to do so. He doesn't require a certain response to grief. He simply walks it with us. Find comfort in where God is leading us. One day we won't wrestle. We won't disappoint. We won't walk in a haze. Rejoice! God is.

"Lord, help me to sing with You."

20

STUCK

Time slows. Your shoulders droop. Legs feel like twenty-ton bricks. Stuck. The inability to move forward. Hardship can immobilize us. We can't find the energy, the mind power, or the will to move forward. In those times, what can we do? This feeling of being stuck often comes from being overwhelmed by our circumstances or past. In His wisdom, God tells us this: "Forget the former things; do not dwell on the past. See, I am doing a new thing!" (Isaiah 43:18 NIV). The first step for us when we can't move is to forget the past. This will sting, but that even means the past that was withheld from us.

In loss, we mourn the loved one and the life we could have had with that person. We can get stuck thinking about what we no longer get to look forward to. All the future Mark and I had planned together. Good plans to honor God, but our plans nonetheless. With Mark in Heaven, I now have to trust God's plans. His good plans for me. We must let go of the one we loved so dearly as well as what could have been. But God tells us He is doing a new thing. We can get out from under the weight of loss and grief by trusting His future for us. Proverbs 4:25-27 (NIV) says it this way: "Let your eyes look straight ahead; fix your gaze directly before you. Give careful thought to the paths for your feet and be steadfast in all your way. Do not turn to the right or the left..." We can't lift the burden of grief from our own chests, but we can fix our eyes on Jesus. Colossians continue this sound advice, extending beyond our eyes: "Set your minds on things above, not on earthly things. For...your life is now hidden with Christ in God" (Colossians 2:2-5 NIV).

I love how God's Word breaks down for us what we can do, step by step, when we can't figure it out. Let go of the past. Look to Jesus. Set your mind on our Savior. Does this work immediately? Sometimes.

Sometimes not. But wherever you find yourself, know that God is with you. And He will rescue you, in His time, in His way. He says, "..for my yoke is easy, my burden light." If you feel stuck under the weight of the world, look up. Think of your Savior. And wait for His saving hand.

"Father, move me forward."

21

ALL DEFENSES ARE DOWN

Hardship can make us feel defenseless. We can't control what is happening. We can't stop the bad news, bad results, or bad future we face. We may not even know where the attack is coming from, much less how to cut it off at the pass. This position can feel helpless and vulnerable. So what can we do? Here is the greatest news! We have a Defender. One that fights for us. What does He expect from us? "The Lord will fight for you; you need only to be still" (Exodus 14:14 NIV). Wait. What? Be still? I can't calm my shaky legs, much less be still. But let's look at where this verse lands in the Bible to understand better what to do when we feel defenseless.

In Exodus, we know the Israelites were set free from Pharoah. This verse is where God tells them to be still. It comes right when they are cornered. The Egyptians were coming behind them. A tremendous body of water was in front of them. In their distress, they asked Moses, "Was it because there were no graves in Egypt that you brought us to the desert to die?" (vs. 11). Ever felt that way? Ever think maybe God was sleeping when your world fell apart? When you get that call? When you came home to nothing? I have been there. Here, in this story of a great exodus, God has them wait on Him. A few things come to the surface as they wait. They see their inability to rescue themselves, and they see God's faithfulness to do the rescuing. Here, by parting the Red Sea and creating a walkway into safety, destroying their enemies. For us, in our grief, it may come in the form of a phone call or voicemail at just the right time or a warm meal delivered in kindness and a listening ear. Whatever it is, it will be from the faithful hand of our Heavenly Father, right on time.

God took Mark Home, healed and well. Peace floods my heart, knowing he is whole and with His Lord and Savior. Yet, I am here in an empty house, heavy with grief.

What happens when you've survived an exodus, only to be cornered by the next attack? What does God do in these verses? He fights for them. He does what He promises He will do, and they are delivered from their attackers, safe and sound, on dry ground. This saving came in their waiting. In His ask of us to wait on Him, we get to see Him swoop in and save us. In grief, it may take some time or even a long time, but grief has no timeline. It's free from the restraints of the clock. And we can find comfort in knowing, however much time it takes, He will show up and make a way for us as we wait on Him.

He fights for us, too. God knows what we cannot do. What amazes me is His great love for us, even in our deficit. He fights when we can't. He defends us when we are defenseless. He loves when we don't love back. He covers us. All of us. All the time. So the next time you feel defenseless, sit still. Call out to Him. Watch him rescue you. He loves you so much!

"Lord, I will be still and watch You fight for me."

22

SPEECHLESS

Oxford defines speechless as "unable to speak, especially as the temporary result of shock or some strong emotion." (Oxford Languages) Relatable. In this day and age, with grief all around, this is a familiar situation we could find ourselves in. Have you ever been driving fast on a highway, and the car two ahead of you darts without warning into the other lane, cutting off those around him and causing panic in every driver between them and you? You watch in disbelief as the car slips past the other cars and no one wrecks. You might drive 5 minutes with no words. Unable to speak. Speechless. Or how about when you get a call from a friend who tells you of a tragedy that happened right in your circle of friends? You hold the phone, breathless, unable to respond. "Hey, you there?" Yeah, you're there, right in the middle of the emotion.

Life does this to us. It can catch our breath and rob us of our words. We lose our ability to communicate our thoughts, feelings, or reactions to the stuff of this life. Sometimes we can't even verbalize our needs when a tragedy happens to us. When word of Mark's diagnosis spread throughout the community, everyone rushed around to help. I had no words. I didn't know how to respond to the shock of our news. I couldn't breathe, much less think to speak.

When we find ourselves speechless it seems impossible to pray or even express our emotions. But we have this Savior who knows our thoughts before we know them (Psalm 139:4). He knows our needs before we do. When we can't understand our circumstances and therefore can't see what we need, Christ Jesus steps in. He does not require words. Only a heart willing to be available to Him. He knows our needs. He is on our side.

So when we find ourselves caught up in the raw emotions of a devastating circumstance, we can rely on and trust that Jesus knows what we need. And He provides. He invites us to "..Casting all your anxiety upon him because he cares for you." (1 Peter 5:7). We don't have to worry when we can't get the words out to ask for His help. He tells us that the Father knows what we need before we ask (Matthew 6:8b). He is with us when we get the call or when we're in those near misses. He is close. And He will provide all we need. Only trust Him.

"Father, I am speechless."

23

UNABLE TO INITIATE

It started in the Garden of Eden, an inability to properly express our need for closeness with our Lord. We got caught up in sin and bogged down in disbelief of our own disappointing choices, and were disconnected from our Creator. What did God do at that moment? "But the Lord God called to the man and said to him, Where are you?" (Genesis 3:9). What does God do today when we cannot initiate a relationship or conversation with Him? When we hide in shame and sorrow? He does the same thing. He calls out to us. He helps us see He is near, even in the heaviness. Even in sorrow. He initiates. We see this truth throughout the Bible. Psalm 139:7-8 poses a scenario where we not only can't initiate but also try to remove ourselves from His presence: "Where shall I go from your Spirit? Or where shall I flee from your presence? If I ascend to heaven, you are there! If I make my bed in Sheol, you are there!"

He pursues us. He knows where we are. He doesn't ask this question in Genesis because He can't find us. He asks this question to help us see clearly that we have moved away from Him. He hasn't moved. Because this life gets so heavy, we sometimes get bogged down and don't even realize we have stopped calling His name. Without realizing that we have shrunk away from our Father, we wonder why we feel so alone and distant.

I found myself stuck in my sunroom once for almost a whole week. I realized I hadn't left the house for several days. Then, I noticed I was spending every waking moment in my sunroom. Isolated. Afraid. Unable to step out into the rest of my life. I felt trapped and unable to move. I could not initiate a change in my surroundings. Then Abba reached in and gently held me close, covering me with His presence, assuring me that He was with me in the sunroom, and in what my family and I were facing. Through His Holy Spirit, He comforted me with His love. I noticed Him in the wind blowing through the trees gently around me, and in the worship music reminding me of His character and steadfast love piping into my sunroom through my phone. He broke through my recoiled frame of mind and recentered me with His truth. Words of truth and peace settled my heart as I let Abba gently comfort me in the quietness of that moment. Alone, yet surrounded by Him. He opened my eyes to see Him, right there, with me.

His love encouraged me to trust Him and step beyond my doubt. He challenged me to step onto the solid rock of His faithfulness and let the truth of who He is steady my footing and my faith. His response to our wandering or distraction is not what some may think. He doesn't stand stiff and out of reach. He presses into us. He reaches down to hold us. Lovingly takes us by the hand and shows He is right there with us. Our creator knows when we can't initiate, and He steps in.

Maybe you can relate to the heaviness or grief. Maybe you can relate to the blockade sin puts up between God and us…or so it seems. When our mind gets cluttered with doubt, remember His promise to never leave us nor forsake us (Deuteronomy, 31:6). Take a moment to write down a verse or two that will refocus your thoughts from doubt and anxiety to the truth of who He is. Start with this one in Deuteronomy:

"Be strong and courageous. Do not fear or be in dread of them, for it is the Lord your God who goes with you. He will be with you; he will never leave you or forsake you. Do not fear or be dismayed."

Tape it to your mirror or near your bedside lamp and tuck it into your purse. Read it out loud whenever you see it. Let His word initiate for you and draw you back into His presence.

"Lord, I can't…"

24

NO RESPONSE

Have you ever been in a situation where you couldn't even respond? Drained. Depleted. Empty. Unable. Stuck emotionally or spiritually with no response? Before grief, I would be hard-pressed to relate to this scenario. However, in deep sorrow, there were many occasions where I stood lacking the ability to reciprocate someone's words, feelings, or ideas expressed.

To reciprocate means to respond to (a gesture or action) by making a corresponding one; or to experience the same (love, affection) for someone as that person does for oneself (Oxford Languages). I met up with a friend of mine who is the salt of the earth. She was attentive and respectful during some difficult times in my husband's diagnosis and battle with cancer. It was my turn to be there for her, as her loved one was recently diagnosed.

I gave her a safe space as we searched for privacy to sit quietly and catch up. She needed a place to be honest and unguarded. She wrestled with admitting that the people in her hometown, who loved and cherished her loved one, were approaching her several times a day to express their concern and get an update on how he was doing. She sheepishly blurted out that though they only had the best intentions, they did not know that with every inquiry, it was as if the scab was being ripped off all over again, and the wound of this diagnosis was fresh and raw. I could relate.

At a time in our journey, I feared going to the grocery store or church. I knew concerned and genuine people would ask, "How is he?" or share their heartfelt concern for him with me. And it ripped off the fragile, thin scar protecting the gaping wound the diagnosis had created within my heart. In those moments, by God's great grace, I would muddle through, thank them for their kindness, and apply pressure to stop the bleeding. I found on those days, it was difficult to dive into my time with the Lord. My soul would honestly pray, "I've given all I can, Father." I felt the walk back to the car was too much. I could sit in His presence, but I could not reciprocate His love, His joy in being with me. I could only sit there. To my surprise and sheer delight, He required no response. He did not expect that I would fake a smile or throw an "I'm good, and You?" insincere, desperate attempt to pretend normalcy His way. He needed nothing from me. He was the one who drew me to Him in the first place. He tells us clearly that even before the world was made, God loved us (Galatians 1:15). Before we could give any response, He loved us. He didn't care that I was unable to hold a conversation with Him. He just sat beside me. What a Savior.

When you are depleted and cannot initiate or reciprocate, He stays beside you with no expectations. In those times, take time to rest, heal, and receive from your loving, all-sufficient Father.

"Lord, I am empty."

25

NO ANSWERS

My dad worked hard in training us to communicate properly. He took the time to teach us how to respond best when being spoken to. You were expected to engage when he spoke to you and answer him immediately with a fitting answer. This took time to learn, and he was patient with us. But soon, he accomplished this goal. As soon as I heard him address me, I would focus on what he was saying, so I could quickly answer him. If I couldn't hear him, I'd move closer to him. If I didn't understand, I would immediately ask questions to give an appropriate answer as soon as possible. But all of that took focus, effort, and determination to stimulate the mind and create the energy to accomplish the task at hand; properly communicating with my dad.

Hardship can rob us of what is needed to communicate properly; focus, effort, and energy. As adults, we can sometimes drift through our day, nodding our heads, smiling when we think that is what is expected, and pretending we are engaged in whatever conversation is trying to rob us of what little energy we have left to give. I've been there before. It can be a very scary feeling, aware that you have no answers for what you are facing. It's almost as if our lives become a dream or vapor of smoke, void of anything sturdy or hardy. We walk in a cloud, and eventually, someone will call our bluff. We will get caught with no answers and no ability to pretend. We must remember in those times that our Father knows our every thought or, at times, the emptiness of our mind. He knows what we need before we ask or even know we have a need. He says in His Word to just ask (Matthew 7:7). In fact, He knows all of the answers, as Father God, the Omniscient One. And He loves us just as we are, void, answerless, empty. He knows us fully and is not shaken by our lack.

Our inability to answer does not affect His love for us. Unlike my dad, who was trying to teach us to communicate and therefore had consequences and practices until we attained the skill, God requires nothing from us. He just wants us to be with Him. To be; a state of being that refers only to the physical.

We can be void of answers in His presence. He already knows what we need, how we feel, and what our minds are trying to process. Let Him be with you. With no expectations. Allow His presence to bring about the healing, rest, acceptance, and love we so desperately need.

"Lord, hear my silence and fill my void."

II.
WHAT HE DOES

There is a kind of suffering that requires help beyond ourselves. We can't reach the ache. We can't see the light. We don't have the power, knowledge, or perspective needed for healing and change. Great news! Our Abba Father does for us what we can't. His intentional love is poured out into our wounded hearts. His unending love and faithfulness bring healing and growth in ways we cannot attain on our own. He knows this. He knows us. And what He does for us is personal to us, His own.

26

HE HEALS US

How often do we let ourselves contemplate the work Christ Jesus accomplished on the cross? You've read Isaiah 53:5 (NIV), "But he was pierced for our transgressions; he was crushed for our iniquities; upon him was the chastisement that brought us peace, and by his stripes, we are healed." The last part of this verse has been quoted as a lifeline of hope for the physically sick. But could it be that we are taking that out of context? We know God cares about our physical health and well-being. The New Testament documents just a tiny portion of all the healing Jesus performed while He walked on Earth. He opened blind eyes, cured leprosy, and raised the dead (Matthew 10:8 is one example of the many healings). Jesus even made time for very personal healings, like the woman "with the issue of blood" for twelve years (Luke 8:43-48).

Jesus cared about our physical illness, no doubt! But He always took His people into deeper, more eternal needs through lessons, parables, and sermons. This portion of scripture in Isaiah is a piece of the foreshadowing of the work Christ was coming to do on the cross for all mankind. He came to save the world. Yes, physical healing is a part of that, but our physical needs are not our greatest need.

There was a turning point in Mark's battle with cancer where his spiritual needs exceeded the physical. I saw him shift from caring for the physical to tending to the spiritual. He was getting his house in order spiritually. We got the call that he only had a little time left. His immediate response was to gather the kids so he could be with each one, speak life and truth into them, and remind them of eternity. His focus moved from what was needed in this world to storing up truths that would firm up our eternal foundation. And I saw peace rushing through him and his words of encouragement. God was showing Mark an even greater need than his need to be healed of cancer in his body. God was bringing about a healing of the soul, for Mark, and myself.

Sin has wedged its way in between our Creator and us and there was a need to be healed spiritually. God loves us so much that He sent his Son (John 3:16) to break through the insurmountable wall of sin and reunite us with Him. The work He did on the cross was to save our souls. Eternally, He healed us by His stripes. Our flesh is temporary. Our souls are eternal.

Jesus knew our greatest need was eternal healing. I saw Mark make that shift in focus as well, as he trusted Christ with his eternity, even as his body was giving up. Though outwardly he was wasting away, inwardly he was being renewed (2 Corinthians 4:16 NIV). We could not take enough supplements, endure enough treatments or surgeries, or heal this sickness in any way whatsoever on our own. None of the best surgeons or specialty doctors could heal the human soul.

Just like Mark's inability to cure himself of cancer, our own sin created the same helpless estate of our soul. No human can save himself. No other sacrifice was sufficient, but the Son of God Himself. So Jesus came, laid His life down, willingly giving it into the hands of those who saw Him as a threat, and by His stripes provided healing for us all. Even His enemies can receive this healing. As we contemplate our need for healing, let's lay it all at His pierced, resurrected feet. Let Him heal you by His stripes. And live!

"Jesus, Thank You for healing my sickness."

27

HE REDEEMS US

As we focus on the word *redeem*, we see it means *to compensate for the faults of (someone or something) or to gain or regain possession (Oxford Languages. languages.oup.com)*. Let's break this definition down to better understand our Savior's act of redemption for each of us. This definition continues with *To compensate for the faults of someone*. That someone is me, and it's you.

I am already aware that I have faults. In fact, many of them. If we're honest, we can all admit this. *To compensate* is crucial in this definition as well. You can interchange it for *exchange*. Christ went to the cruel cross and exchanged His life for yours; for mine. He took our place. *To gain or regain possession*. He who created us sent His Son. Christ died in exchange for our lives, *regaining* us as His own.

This truth especially permeated my mind in the middle of my grief. Knowing that Christ loved me to the point of His own death brought all my questions and pain into a different light. That He was willing to die on the cross for me reminded me that He loves me, even when I didn't feel His love. Even when I felt nothing but the loss of my husband. Jesus loved me. And because of this truth, I was not alone. It also brought light into my grief knowing that Mark was with Redeemer and all his needs were being met by this same Jesus.

As I mourned Mark's death here on earth, Jesus was giving him a new body, healing every hurt Mark had ever felt, and welcoming him into Heaven. This was possible because Christ went to the cross, exchanged Mark's life for His own, and poured His righteousness over Mark, making a way for him to be in heaven with God when Mark left this earth. All of this was possible because Christ redeemed him. There is an indescribable peace in this truth. Mark is reunited with Christ in Heaven!

All of us who have accepted Christ as our Savior have been reunited with Him and one day we too will be face-to-face. In His death and resurrection, He has regained us. What currency was used? Money? No. Something much more binding and valuable. "For you know that it was not with perishable things such as silver or gold that you were redeemed from the empty way of life handed down to you by your ancestor, but with the precious blood of Christ, a lamb without blemish or defect" 1 Peter 1:18-19 (NIV). Without blemish or defect validates the exchange. The only One worthy sacrificed His life for our own. And now we are His. And why does He redeem us? For His glory. Psalm 111:6-9 says, "...He has shown the people the power of His works...The works of his hands are faithful and just; all his precepts are trustworthy. They are established forever and ever, enacted in faithfulness and uprightness. He provided redemption for his people; he ordained his covenant forever holy, and awesome is his name."

As we walk through grief, we can find such rich comfort in knowing that this exchange reunites us with our Lord and Savior, and we can look forward to being reunited with those who go before us, who have accepted this redemption from the Savior of all mankind. When your heart is heavy, let this truth shed light and hope in your grief. We have a place, redeemed by Christ's blood, forever in paradise with Him.

"Lord, I am Yours."

28

HE CALLS US

When we struggle through trials, we must remember that our struggle has a purpose. God does not allow difficulty without a reason. I like to envision a baby chick breaking open its hard shell. This newborn is weak, fragile, and even thin-skinned. Yet it must break through this shell. This fragile, tired chick was designed by its Creator to endure this struggle. You'll agree if you've been privileged to see this beautiful battle for freedom. It's almost as if its Creator is cheering it on. "You can do this. I'm right here. Almost there." As the chick emerges, there is almost a sigh of relief heard as the last of the shell falls away. He has a purpose for the chicken in the egg to struggle. He has a plan for our struggle as well. Do not lose heart. He is leading us somewhere in our difficult times.

In hardship, He leads us closer to Him. He calls us to Him. He will use our difficult situation to draw us in. But don't miss that He calls us to Himself *in* the struggle. This very book is a result of God calling me in my grief and sorrow, to take all He has taught me, honor Him, and share my story. He has called me to float beside Him, observe all He is doing, and proclaim to all who will listen. He is faithful, and He uses our struggle for His glory. Where is God when we are facing hardship? He is right beside us. We see evidence of this throughout the Word of God. Psalms 23:4 shows us, "Even though I walk through the valley of the shadow of death, I will fear no evil, for you are with me." Never in my life had the words of this psalm touched me more profoundly than when I was sitting alone in my grief, alone in a home that I once shared with my life partner. God was there, in the hurt and confusion, sorrow and utter loss. I missed Mark, but I was not alone. I have never been alone at any point in my life. And because I never walk alone, I can stand unafraid of whatever comes at me in this valley. In the darkest times, He is there. He calls us to Himself, to walk with Him in the valleys and on the mountaintops. And in our grief, there will be difficulties we face, yet we never face them alone.

Sometimes the hardship is so big we forget He has a plan, a purpose, and that He's calling us to His side. When the struggle gets to be too much, we can get rattled. Let's settle our hearts with this practice David teaches us when things get tough. "I have set the Lord continually before me; Because He is at my right hand, I will not be shaken" (Psalm 16:8 NIV). First, we see the invitation to seek Him continuously. Then we see the reality of David living this out amid hardship. He calls us *in* the struggle, and He uses the struggle to draw us closer to Him. As we face trials, let's keep our minds set on His call for us to be at His side. Let's rejoice over His desire to have us near Him.

"Lord, I hear You. Keep me by Your side."

29

HE TEACHES US

"I will instruct you and teach you in the way you should go; I will counsel you with my loving eye on you" (Psalm 32:8). David has been taught by God his whole life. From the field to the palace. From being ignored to being popular. From shepherd to king. God instructed him through the lonely times when he feared for his life. And in the times when he was rejoicing in the spoils of all the victories God had led him into. It's safe to say God taught David through it all. He does the same for us today. Some of what we go through feels useless, painful, or unredeemable. Yet God is known for turning ugly into beautiful.

Joseph was a son of Jacob and went through hardship. His brothers hated him. They sold him into slavery. He was lied about and eventually imprisoned. Yet at the end of his story, God made him second in command to Pharaoh, a position of great worth for Egypt and the Israelite Nation. All of his hardship positioned him to save Israel from famine. With every new struggle, every letdown, or moment he felt forgotten, God was developing character, and strengthening Joseph's faith in his God. Joseph grew to know and trust that his God was able and faithful to take ashes and turn them into beauty. To take what was meant to harm and use it for good.

We can peek into the story of Esther to see that she, too, was a student of God's. Her story starts out grim. She had no parents in a culture that did not favor her nationality. Yet at the end of her story, the Jewish nation is again saved! God does that. He takes bad circumstances and turns them into great ones. And He teaches us along the way. An outcast becomes the leader of a mighty nation. An orphan learns how to be a spokesperson and a queen. God is always teaching us.

I love the reminder in Psalm 25:12 that God even teaches us in our sins: "Good and upright is the Lord; Therefore, he instructs sinners in the way." It is out of His goodness that He teaches us. Great news! It's not dependent on us. It's what He does. In His teaching, our hardship has a purpose. His teaching helps us shift our thinking in difficult times to the promise that God is working things out for our good, as we trust Him and are called according to His purpose (Romans 8:28). A shift in thinking to things that are lovely, noble, good (Philippians 4:8) can make all the difference in our hard times. He teaches us not because we deserve or earn it. No. He teaches us because He loves us. We are His children. We need only receive His teaching. Job pleads with his friends, "Please receive instruction from His mouth and establish His words in your heart" (Job 22:22).

We can turn away from God when things get tough, or, with an open heart, we can receive His instruction with a good outcome in the works. I have done both. One leads to more heartache. The other leads us to His arms and peace. Let Him teach you today. Be still. Listen to His instruction. He is doing good through your difficulties.

"Father, teach me."

30

HE REFINES US

Have you ever seen a silversmith working with precious metals? This ancient trade has been used for hundreds of years to bring about ageless treasures. This refining process mirrors what our Father in Heaven does with us. It starts with precious metal, but work must be done to get it ready to be perfect. The silver must be put into the fire, where dross and other impurities are extracted. The metal is shaped and then put back in the fire. This process is repeated until the metal can withstand the test of durability. It becomes so refined that the Silversmith can see his reflection in the finished product.

Do you feel like you've been in the fire? Hardship can do that. For my family, it seemed to never end. The pressure of keeping those around us informed, trying to maintain as much normalcy for the kids' lives as possible, and getting on our knees, surrendering it all to Abba, seemed like a nonstop refining method. We'd try on our own and fail. Ask forgiveness. Return to His side. Then something would happen, and we'd start all over again. We'd squirm under the pressure and end up relying on our own strength, which, of course, failed.

The interesting thing about the precious metal is that it does not squirm or attempt escape. It's not a living thing, so there is no battle. We, however, can battle. We can resist the intense heat. Or trust that we are in good hands.

Psalm 66:10-12 tells us that God tries his people. "For you have tried us, O God; you have refined us as silver is refined. You brought us into the net; you laid an oppressive burden upon our loins. You made men ride over our heads; we went through fire and water, yet you brought us out into a place of abundance." God allows hardship in our lives to refine us. To pull out the dross and pull us closer to Him. And where we end up is always a place of abundance. His kingdom is multiplied through our testimony. He uses our story to show others His reflection.

Look at Job. Tested by God. He battled. He struggled. He endured much hardship. Loss. Sickness. Abandonment. Yet, in the end, we could see God's reflection shining through him. And we still talk about his story today. In Zechariah 13:9, we read, "And I will put this third in the fire, and test them as gold is tested. They will call upon My Name, and I will answer them. I will say, 'They are my people,' and they will say, 'The Lord is my God.'" His goal is to pull out impurities and stumbling blocks and call us His own. He's been in the refining business since the first man. He knows what He is doing.

We can resist and fight against His gentle, skilled hand. Or we can trust that He won't let the fire consume us. We can lean into what the refining hand of Abba Father is producing within us - a stronger faith in Him and the courage to let Him do the hard work within us so we can stand firmly on what He tells us in His Word. This process redirects our doubt with His truth by intentionally putting scripture into our minds when we feel doubt creeping into our hearts. And proclaiming out loud that He is faithful and is working in our hearts and minds to bring about His glory will allow us to remember that He is for us and with us. And the finished product? We will shine for Him and reflect His image to others. Let's let our refining reveal the goodness of our Loving Savior.

"Lord, refine me."

31

HE FORGIVES US

Haven't we all longed for forgiveness? We all need it. We all fall short. Scripture tells us this, but we already know, don't we? We sin. Sometimes blatantly. Sometimes honestly. And we need forgiveness. This is true on our best days and when we are in the throes of hardship. I used to think God would just forgive me when I sin in hardship. He gets it, right? I've come to learn that because He gets it, He still requires repentance, even in grief. Taking a closer look at forgiveness helps us see its gift and necessity.

Forgiveness is God removing our sin and erasing it from us. Sin is such a heavy burden. The enemy doesn't call a timeout in our hardship and offers comfort with no strings attached. He is always out to kill, steal, and destroy (John 10:10). God knows this. He invites us to be free from the burden of our sins. Philippians 4:6 says it this way, "do not be anxious for anything, but in everything, by prayer and petition, with thanksgiving, present your requests to God." To present our requests to God allows an intimate exchange between the Creator and the created. One that Abba Father always welcomes. He wants us to bring our anxiety and let Him turn it into faith. That is what bringing all our needs to Him does. Only God can do that.

So, when we are tempted in our hardship to sin, what if we present our request to God? What if we reach for Abba Father instead? 1 Peter 5:7 shows God's heart towards us. He instructs us to "Cast all your cares on him because he cares for us." He cares for us on our good and bad days. He knows that in hardship, we need relief because He also knows what sin costs. He demands that we confess our sins and not overlook them because He knows what sin does. It eats at our souls, minds, and bodies. He offers forgiveness because it's what we need. He promises if we confess, He will forgive and cleanse us! (1 John 1:9). Do you hear His heart in this invitation? "I already know, Child. I know what this sin is doing to you. Let me take it. Let me lighten your load." This is what Abba Father says to us. Proverbs 28:13 says, "Whoever conceals his transgressions will not prosper, but he who confesses and forsakes them will obtain mercy." Instead of more hardship from sin, let's receive mercy.

Take His invitation in Isaiah to heart, "'Come, let us discuss this,' says the Lord. 'Though your sins are like scarlet, they will be as white as snow; though they are as red as crimson, they will be like wool'" (1:18 HCSB). This is the heart of God. He knows us. He knows sin. He knows the truth about tolerating any of it. Exchanging sin for a false sense of comfort utterly destroys us. It gives the illusion of hope, peace, or healing but what it really does is drive us away from God and causes us to turn to other things that cannot help us. He loves us too much to look the other way. God saves. That is who He is. He invites us to sit down with Him and share our sorrows and needs and then He pours into us His Spirit, like a healing balm, and cleanses us as only God can. His cleansing of our sins brings true healing and draws us closer to our Lord and Savior.

"Lord, I confess. Cleanse me."

32

HE UNITES US

Unity is bringing together while isolation is remaining alone. I know in hardship, there is a great temptation to isolate. We're exhausted. Our mind is not focused on the current events of this world or even on what's happening in our living room. What does God do in our hardship? He brings us into unity with Himself through His Holy Spirit. 1 Corinthians 6:17 says, "he who is joined to the Lord is one spirit with Him." This is crucial in our struggle to know and believe we are never alone. He is with us always. Matthew 28:20b says, "... to the ends of the earth." This includes the end of our sorrow and pain in this life. Jesus unites us with God Almighty. We know we are united with Christ, His Holy Spirit, and God through the teachings on the vine and branches found in John 15:5-8. I have found profound comfort in this truth, especially in my hardship. The enemy wants us to isolate ourselves. It's in our aloneness that Satan deceives us into thinking we have no one, no hope, no relief. He can heap blame, shame, and lies on us when there is no one around to counter him.

I struggled with having to send my kids to stay with other families while I tended to Mark's needs. At times I felt like I was failing them as a mom. I wrestled with the guilt of being unable to be in two places simultaneously. The enemy would get me down and make me feel like I wasn't doing anything well. God's Word reminded me that He is with my family and me in hard times. And when I aligned my thoughts with Him, the isolation left, and hope was restored. Being united brings hope, relief, and truth.

The truth is God will never leave us. He will never forsake us. His word proclaims that again and again. In our hardship, we are united with God Almighty, His Son, Jesus, and the Holy Spirit, the Great Comforter.

Taking time to sit in His presence, open His Word, and meditate on it, brings peace. It brings truth. When we are one with Him, we have His strength, insight, wisdom, and Him with us. Facing our hardship with Him gives us hope and strength. Facing it in isolation defeats us and brings us down. We know one of the ways God connects with us is through His Church. In grief, reaching out or even opening your door is hard. May I suggest letting one or even two friends into your hardship? This will connect you to God and others as well. Both are crucial in difficult times because of the tactics of the enemy. In isolation, from God or others, we are vulnerable to depression and a feeling of hopelessness and defeat. When we connect with God and with others, there is a sense of togetherness that lifts our spirits and ushers in hope.

The tangible presence of a fellow believer can do wonders for encouraging and strengthening a hurting soul. Let someone you trust and know loves Jesus into your home or even just into your thoughts. A short visit or phone call can lift us up and refresh us. Sharing what we're going through with others allows them to better carry this burden with us. It could be a meal, a scripture verse, or just a listening ear.

Taking time to sit quietly with the Lord, even to meditate briefly on one verse, also lifts us up and reminds us that He is always with us and He never leaves us. We are not alone. We were made to be in unity with God and each other. In your struggle, consider letting someone in. Watch and see how God's promises come to life. Let others help keep your eyes fixed on the Author and Perfecter of our faith as your faith is tested in hardship. Stop the enemy in his attempt to isolate, deceive, and weary you. Walk in the unity God provides, and be encouraged.

"Lord, unify me with Yourself and others today."

33

HE FIGHTS FOR US

We are not alone in our battles. We have a defender. God is our defender. He is mighty and righteous. He comes to our defense. He calls us to be still. To be silent, even. Where is the Lord when we are fighting? Exodus 14:14 says, "The Lord will fight for you, and you have only to be silent." He is the One fighting on our behalf. The value of knowing this truth in our hardship is immeasurable.

We've all been in a place where we feel no one is with us as we face hardship. We feel alone. The truth is that we are not. We can rest in His promises and know that our God is active in our defense. After Mark went Home, I felt so alone. We were such a team in our marriage, with our kids, in our lifework. And all I could see was the loneliness. I knew God was with me, but I struggled to understand this practically. I felt like every day was a battle. Simple tasks seemed insurmountable for me. As I sat on my porch one evening, weary and defeated, I grabbed His Word and read the truth about my circumstances. In Deuteronomy 20:4, we hear, "For the Lord God is he who goes with you to fight for you against your enemies, to give you the victory." We have this assurance that He will fight for us and win for us. Although I had no physical enemies, I felt the enemy of my soul pressing in, attempting to isolate and defeat me in my spirit. Can you relate to that feeling? David could. He penned this truth about how God responds to us in our time of need. "When the righteous cry for help, the Lord hears them and delivers them out of all their troubles" (Psalm 34:7). David is writing this as a declaration of his personal experience. Even David needed to be rescued.

We see throughout this psalm the security we have in letting God fight for us. David says in verse 8, "Oh, taste and see that the Lord is good! Blessed is the man who takes refuge in Him!" As we trust the Lord and seek our refuge in Him there will be blessings. He hears us! And He will answer our cries for help. We still battle. We still go through hardship on this earth, but we know who has brought us victory. 1 Corinthians 15:57 is very clear about this truth: "But thanks be to God who gives us the victory through our Lord Jesus Christ."

When we focus on our Victor, it clarifies what our role is in hardship. To be still. We know He will bring us victory. It's who He is and what He does. There is none above Him. It's also true that He is on our side. He is for us. When we feel the battle, it is clear who fights for us and what is required of us. He will fight. We need only be still. Let Him war on your behalf.

In your stillness, you can cry out to Him. Tell Him your fears, share your anger, and make known to Him your concerns. Like David, share your fears and needs with Him. And in your crying out, be encouraged that He is actively fighting your battle. He hears and He responds. He fights and brings us the victory. Trust Him today with your hardship.

"Lord, I will trust and be still."

34

HE VALIDATES US

Hardship has a way of rattling our identity. It can cause us to question who we are. How strong we are. What are we made of. I am familiar with these doubts. But this train of thought focuses on us, our abilities, and our strength. We will always come up short-handed. Why? Because we are limited humans. Instead of drilling ourselves when we face things too difficult for us, let's look at what God thinks of us.

Scripture is full of evidence of how God views us. He knows we fall short (Romans 3:23). When we fall short, He fills us with more of Himself. He shows us who we are in Him. This perspective changes everything. First, we are sinners. This is important to note because if we don't come to this realization, we won't see our need for a Savior. Hardship has a way of showing us our needs. This is a good thing. Struggles break down our pride. We see ourselves as not enough. But what does God do in this awareness? He tells us who we are, His children. One of my favorite verses is 1 John 3:1. Listen to how God defines us in this verse, "See what great love the Father has lavished on us, that we should be called children of God! And that is what we are!" (1 John 3:1a NIV). Do you hear the excitement within John as he pens this?

God calls us His own! He tells us we are His children! We can go back to Genesis to see how God validates us. In Genesis 1:27, He tells us that we are made in His image. He chose us. We are His, made to look like Him, much like a son looks like his dad or mom. Sometimes our kids don't act like us exactly, not until they mature and grow in wisdom, but they still bear our image. There is a family resemblance. We resemble the Holy Father of all life! That is who we are. On our sunny days and our struggles. It will give us a new perspective if we set our minds on this truth.

This truth changes the way we face tough times. We know who we are based on His Word. We know who we are. We belong to Him. And it's through this adoption that we have access to God's strength, wisdom, and any other resource needed to walk through our trials victorious. Strong. Capable (Galatians 4:5-7). Not pulling from ourselves. Rather, pulling from our Father in Heaven. Today, as you meditate on His truth, let Him validate who you are in Christ. Let Him point out untruths you are believing about yourself and replace them with the truth of who He says you are. Look up a verse or two on who He says you are. Let His words validate you. Maybe even jot a verse or two down in your journal to remind yourself as needed. Accept His truth of who you are, and be at peace.

"Lord, confirm me as Your own."

35

HE AFFIRMS US

There are two definitions for the word *affirm*. The first one is to speak as a fact, strongly and publicly, the truth in a matter. (Oxford Languages) It is truth spoken with authority from the one who knows confidently, without any doubt. The other definition is to offer emotional support or encouragement (Oxford Languages). We have a bad habit of trying to affirm the truth about ourselves through the wrong sources. We look to people, our emotions, our circumstances, or the stars above. Don't get me wrong. There is something so amazing in words of encouragement from the ones we know, trust, and love. It's one of the Five Love Languages (Gary Chapman's Five Love Languages). There is only One who has the authority to speak the truth about us. He knows who we are whether we are doing things well or not, living our best life or not. The one source of truth in who we truly are is God. We are to look to our Creator, Savior, God, and not rely on any other source, for our affirmation.

As humans, the authority to affirm ourselves or those around us doesn't come from ourselves. It comes from the One who made us, who knit us together in our mother's womb (Psalm 139:13). The One who knew us before the foundations of the earth were laid (Ephesians 1:4). He alone has the authority to speak truth over you with unquestionable authority. By His Spirit living in us, we stand validated. My husband would say these verses aloud many times during our battle, as the enemy would try to discourage and confuse us in our identity. Before the foundations of the earth were laid, God knew and saw us here. We can rest in this truth. It became a daily confirmation for us both, sometimes in total opposition to our feelings and what we were seeing before our eyes. And in those times, this truth coming from our Maker brought us back into His care and His truth.

1 Peter 2:9 tells us what God affirms about us, "But you are a chosen race, a royal priesthood, a holy nation, a people for his own possession, that you may proclaim the excellencies of him who called you out of darkness into his marvelous light." Here, God is talking to the Israelite people whom He chose to be set apart from the rest of the world. He chose a people to show the world who He is, that He is the One true God, and that He engages with people, His created. We also know that when Christ came, we who believed in His name and confessed with our mouths that Jesus is Lord have been adopted into this chosen people, God's family (Ephesians 1:5). His affirmation of us is unconditional. It doesn't change when we are struggling with the stuff of this life or when we struggle with the truth itself.

"Lord, remind me of Your love for me today.

36

HE COMMISSIONS US

We've all heard of The Great Commission in the Bible, where Jesus commands his disciples to go and tell the Gospel to everyone, right? (Matthew 28) I know you're thinking, "What does that have to do with hardship?" A few things happened when Christ gave this command to his disciples. Let's look at them.

When we read these powerful verses in the Bible, we must look at what had just happened and the condition of the disciples emotionally and mentally. Their Savior had just been privately and illegally judged, publically dragged through the streets, openly humiliated by all, and then horrifically killed. By association, they were also humiliated and felt like they had been dragged through the streets. They were exhausted. Terrified. Depleted.

Sound like grief to anyone? They were grieving in the upper room, huddled together behind a locked door. I can certainly relate to this position in my own grief. The last thing I wanted to do was have a heavy conversation with someone else outside of our family. The stress of our hardship seemed to take too much out of me. And yet, I didn't want to miss an opportunity to be the light to someone around me. Just as Christ equipped the disciples He had called, He equips us too. Even in hardship. They were given a task to get to the mountain where Jesus had told them to go. I can only imagine their mental and emotional state. Yet, they mustered up the courage to obey their Master. They arrived. They met with Jesus, as He said they would. They were given a new task; Go and tell the world about Me (Matthew 28:19). Through Christ, they were equipped to share the story of the One True Savior. This tells us that Jesus was not only aware but familiar with their strife, sorrow, and lack. In knowing this, did Jesus say, "Goodness, you need to go hide for a while?" No, He didn't.

There was a day I was trying to reach out and be present outside of my family, and it was so difficult. I showed up to a Bible study, struggled through it, and went right back home. The next week I got a text from a woman in the throes of a terrible divorce. She simply said, "Your presence there gave me hope. Thank you." If we are willing, He will use us. Jesus used the disciples in their hardship too. He knew what they were feeling and thinking and commissioned them to go. Right there, in their grief and hardship. True, they saw Him alive again. But that didn't fix all the ripple effects of His death for them. They still lived in a region where they would be hated and mocked. The message itself could cost them their lives, and eventually, it did. In the middle of the hardship, Jesus commissioned them to go and do His will. He does the same for us, but not without a promise. "And behold, I am with you always, to the end of the age" (Matthew 28:20b). Knowing Christ is with us always, even in our grief and sorrow, let's ask Him for the strength to obey and be willing to be used right here, in our hardship.

"Lord, send me, even in my grief."

37

HE RESTORES US

"The Lord is my shepherd, I shall not want... He restores my soul" (Psalm 23:1, 3a). This psalm has been used by many as a source of comfort. It's also been nicknamed "the Funeral Psalm." But in my grief, Abba Father shed new light on it. Instead of this being a psalm read at funerals, He showed me it is a psalm proclaiming the provision of our Abba Father in real-time hardship. It moves from end-of-life application to everyday encouragement. In the decade of the battle my family endured, where the threat of cancer, sickness, and even death was so prevalent, God brought me to this 23rd Psalm so many sleepless nights. He began to show me His ever-presence and tender care for His own in the most trying times. Sleepless nights where worry and anxiety pushed their way into my personal space and set up residency in my heart. I was retreating to my sunroom and spending more time in there than with the Lord. I admitted to my husband that I struggled to cross the threshold, reentering our house as I knew what battles awaited me. The concerned phone calls. The well-meaning neighbors. The unanswered messages from the kids' schools. I was lost in grief, with worry and anxiety calling the shots. That was my perception but not the truth. The truth? I have a Good Shepherd.

As my Shepherd, the things coming into my life are managed by the Almighty. In grief, these tender verses come to life with a realness that carries us through the darkest nights and the deepest valleys. We are all aware of the comforts this world offers. The gamut of things to distract us, from entertainment to indulgence, is neverending. As Christians, we are told to come to Him, and He will give us rest (Matthew 11:28). I have known this to be true. And still, I have turned to other things, only to be left empty-handed. Running to a friend first before I run into God's arms has left me wanting. They mean well, but are not familiar with my specific troubles, as my Comforter is. Numbing my mind in an attempt to escape grief only lasts for a moment. When I shut the TV off I am still void and lacking, and now with wasted hours to process. These other things may not even be bad but they cannot restore my weary soul. Only He can give me the rest I seek.

Yet, there are times when we cannot find rest. So what does the Father do for us in these times? He restores our souls. In our distress, with good intentions, we can find ourselves running to other things for comfort. We set out with God's Word in hand and worship fresh on our lips, and then we get knocked off the path. We grab the first thing that floats by; music, TV, a substance that lets us escape. It is an imitation of comfort, and we briefly slip away from our hardship. But when the temporary comfort is gone, we are no more replenished than before. Jesus spoke to us about this false comfort when He proclaimed, "Peace I leave with you; my peace I give you. I do not give as the world gives" (John 14:27).

Christ's restoration comes with no strings attached and no hidden agenda. He knows our souls. He created us. And what He gives is real, lasting, and rich in life. Psalm 23 reminds us that only He can restore our souls. We can turn to the world and try its quick fixes, but they will always leave us empty-handed and wanting. Today, if you're depleted, run-down, or without, receive comfort from your Savior. Let Him restore your soul.

"Lord, restore my soul."

38

HE HIDES US

It was a particularly difficult day. We had gotten test results back and had a follow-up visit with the surgeon. The leg had to come off. Mark and I were still reeling in the reality of what was now our new challenge when we had to swing by the grocery store. We decided to go in together, as Mark knew I was shaky from the day's events. He was hurting but thinking of me. Before we stepped out of the car, he gently grabbed my arm and said, "Tina, God's got us. He is our safe place. Let's pray." As my eyes filled with tears, Mark asked God to cover us and be the strength within us as we faced the grocery store and our kids later that evening with this heartbreaking news. I just wanted to be invisible, get what we needed, and get home. I cringed at the thought of running into someone and hearing, "How are things going with you, Mark?" God protected us from a heavy confrontation and guided our steps through the store, through the checkout line, and into our vehicle. Somehow we were able to get what we needed quickly and quietly.

The kids were rattled when we sat down to share the new plan. But as we sat together, under the arms of the Almighty, we resolved to love each other and be the light through this, by God's strength.

Sometimes we are in over our heads. We can't find the strength. Our circumstances leave us raw and vulnerable. We want to keep shining for our Heavenly Father, but we are tapped out. We need a safe place to breathe, soak in our reality, and be reminded of God's truth. What does God do for us in those times? He covers us with His favor as with a shield (Psalm 5:12). He infuses us with His strength, which never runs out and is greater than any other source. We may still feel shaky and even helpless on our own, but here's the thing: We are never on our own. In these times, God hides us in His love, and He covers us with His wings and provides a hiding place when we need it (Psalm 32:7).

The temptation is to face these difficult times alone, in our own strength. If it's a long battle, like ours was, there is a sense of using up His mercy and the threat of it running out. We think, "We've called on Abba so much lately. Let's handle this on our own." But that is not what He calls us to do, and that is impossible. He never runs out of love, mercy, strength, or help. And we can't do these things on our own. We will face things out of our control. He knows this about His children. We may even need a hiding place. He provides that. Abba Father delights in providing the rest we need.

When you find yourself shaky, unstable, and needing a place to be invisible, go to Him. Let Abba hide you in His arms. He is our strong tower. Run to Him and be safe (Proverbs 18:10). He promises to always be there for you. You will find the rest and strength you need for each moment in Him.

"Lord, hide me."

39

HE RESCUES US

Remember the part in the movie "The Avengers" where the heroes swoop in at the last minute and save the day? They battle, are victorious, and save everyone on Earth from the bad guys in space. The enemy was big, scary, and more powerful than any one of them, but then The Avengers came to the rescue and somehow pulled out the win, and the world was saved from their enemies. I know, that's only a movie. But guess what? We have One who rescues us!

In 2 Samuel 22:18, David documents God's faithful rescue from his enemies. "He rescued me from my strong enemy...." In fact, David dedicates this entire psalm to the mighty hand of God, his Victor! We share the same Victor today.

Throughout our battle with cancer, I can't count the times my family needed to be rescued. Rescued from the horror of a cancer diagnosis. Rescued from the lasting effects, physically and mentally, of chemo. Rescued from taking our eyes off of Jesus and trying to understand things in our own strength. Rescued from the vicious attacks of satan whispering lies and attempting to snuff our faith in our Lord and Savior right out.

It was a battle not just for Mark, who had the diagnosis, but for myself and our four kids. It was brutal. We felt crushed under the weight of it all. Crushed, maybe, but never destroyed (2 Corinthians 4:8-9). How can this be? By His strength, not our own (Exodus 15:2). In hard times, it's easy to forget that the God of the Universe is for us. He is on our side. He is an ever-present help in our times of need (Psalm 46:1).

It's easy to forget, but it never wavers in being the truth. Our circumstances are in His hands at all times. And like a loving, perfect

Father, when we need Him, He is there. Scriptures tell us, "All who call on the Name of the Lord will be saved" (Romans 10:13). In Psalm 69, David calls out again, asking for God's rescue. "Deliver me from sinking in the mire; let me be delivered from my enemies and from the deep waters" (vs. 14). In this psalm, we see real live enemies that we need to be rescued from, as well as circumstances, those deep waters that creep up and cover our heads. There were times my family felt this. Drowning in the ripple effects of cancer.

Regardless of our emotions, circumstances, or fleeting strength, the truth of His promises remains. Call out to Abba and let Him rescue you today. As He did for David, He will do for you. He is the same mighty God. When you feel covered up, or surrounded by enemies, cry out to God and, like David, be rescued.

"Lord, rescue me."

40

HE ADOPTS US

I am undone by the generosity of God the Father who chose us. Not only that, He lavished us with His love and adopted us into His family. This is a fascinating truth we can rest our weary heads on. Paul tells us in Romans 8:15-17 that we "have received a spirit of adoption, through which we cry 'Abba, Father!'" We can bank our very identity in this scripture. God drives this truth home in several places in His Word. Ephesians tells us we are chosen by God to be adopted into His family (Ephesians 1:3-6). John 1:12-13 goes even further. We have been given the right to become children of God. That goes beyond a want or wish. And further still, "we have received the spirit of adoption, by which we cry, 'Abba! Father!'" (Romans 8:14-17).

As His children, we have access to Him as Daddy. Romans 9:8 even takes away the need to earn this title as sons and daughters within our own ability. We are the direct result of God keeping His promise to Abraham. We are His because He chose us. We are His because He made a way for us to become His. He makes us worthy and gives us this title.

In the throes of our battle with cancer, I noticed that our family started strong in their faith. But with each blow to the gut, each bad scan, and each discovery of more cancer, what faded was not our faith in God. Rather, it was our faith in our identity. We began to question if we were still His children. I found myself thinking, "Maybe I am just not really His child." My brain could not comprehend a Father who was all-powerful and sovereign, allowing such heart-wrenching things to happen to His daughter.

It's crazy how twisted the enemy's lies can become. These lies get us to question not the Almighty God, but who we are in Him. It took me a while to see this tactic of the enemy. Once God showed me, I surrendered and confessed it to Abba. He graciously corrected the misunderstanding. Once He showed me all these places in His Word where He has addressed our adoption into His family, I realized a few things.

First, I saw that I am not the only one who has struggled with this. It is in His Word too many times for it to be a "me only" problem. Another thing I realized through the truth of my identity is that Abba is a good, good Father. As His child, I can walk through horrible hardships and be secure in Him. Like a good dad, He carries, shields, and strengthens us with truth.

When you get covered up in difficult circumstances, and you forget who you are, press into His Word. It's everywhere! We are adopted into His family.

"Abba, Thank You. I am Yours."

41

HE AVENGES US

There's a difference between *revenge* and *avenge*. This matters because God tells us plainly in Deuteronomy 32:35, "It is mine to *avenge*; I will repay, says the Lord." When we are less concerned with justice and more concerned with retaliating by inflicting harm we seek revenge. As humans, we tend to forget justice when we've been harmed. We want the other person to hurt like they hurt us.

My husband had to get a port put in for the chemo to be administered. This device was surgically implanted into his neck. He asked the nurse if having a port put in hurt, to which she nonchalantly replied, "Not really." After the procedure, Mark couldn't believe how much pain his neck was in. When she returned to check on him, he told her she was wrong and that the port really did hurt. She flippantly said, "You're about to undergo some really painful chemo. It's time to put on your big boy panties and brace yourself." I was so livid I couldn't speak. I wanted to find her most vulnerable place and drive harsh words into it. Mark was already uncertain and nervous. She was so callous and indifferent to my hurting husband. I wanted her to hurt like she hurt him. That is the human response.

Issuing revenge only breeds more hurt. God responds differently. He tells us that He will make it right when others harm us. He will avenge us and punish the wrong as He also brings about justice. See the difference? We just want to lash out when we are hurt. God wants justice to be done.

When we struggle, we see things through hurt eyes. I saw that nurse as a nasty, hard-hearted lady. But God saw her heart. He knew her. He knew why she treated a cancer patient that way. He knew if she was responding from a place of hurt or just being ugly and indifferent. He sees all. He knows all. He alone can make all things right. And justice will be done in His time. I am learning that only God can see the heart of someone (Proverbs 21:2). We can't know and see all. I am also learning that we see through partial eyes. We focus on ourselves, not others. We can't help ourselves. It is the limited, selfish flesh. But God is impartial (Romans 2:11), and therefore He alone can truly avenge. It's important to know this about ourselves when we are in hardship. It's even more important to trust that God, the only one able to avenge, will act on our behalf. He will make all things right one day. We can rest assured of this. If you find yourself being unjustly treated or just plain hurt, rest in this promise from God. Try to hold back the desire to lash out, causing more hurt. Say a prayer for them, and let God handle it.

"Lord, avenge me."

42

HE CLEANSES US

I rounded the corner of the cluttered hallway and found a laundry room full of sweaty gym shorts, muddy cleats, and gym bags that could get up and walk right out of the house. Every week, I was met with a new challenge of how to get some foreign goop out of uniforms. Sometimes I won the battle. Other times, they showed up on the court with a clear reminder that some things were beyond my ability. I was not up on the laundry in our battle with cancer. I wasn't as prepared for the game day turnaround. It bothered me because I felt like my family looked unprepared and sometimes even a little dirty. Hardship can do that. We do our best, but things start to slip. And we show our inability.

My shortcomings and distractions helped me realize no matter how much you seem to have it all together, there is a cleansing no human can do for themselves. The stain of sin is impenetrable. No secret recipe or magic product can do what God's Son's blood has accomplished for us. And no mom, even SuperMom, can wipe away the sins of the human soul. Oh, praise Him, His blood is enough. I have always found enormous comfort in this verse in Isaiah: "'Come now, let us reason together,' says the Lord. 'Though your sins are like scarlet, they shall be as white as snow; though they are red like crimson, they shall become like wool'"(Isaiah 1:18). Here, God is talking to the Israelites. They repeatedly disobeyed, turned from His Word, and got their uniforms covered with stains. Like my kids' stained uniforms, the Israelites continued growing their mountain of stains. What hope was there for the Israelites? What hope is there for us?

I love the NIV version of this verse. It says, "Let us settle the matter..." God's promises settle the matter of guilt, sin, and shame for our dirty laundry. So no matter if we are the mom who has it all together or we can't find a clean matching sock, God has our backs. He cleanses us. Not because we somehow have managed to stay on top of everything in our grief and hardship. Not because we have done anything. He cleanses us because He said He would.

Regardless of what is going on in our lives. Regardless of how we are or aren't handling it. He loves us. And He washes our sins away. David calls out to God and asks of Him, "Purify me with hyssop, and I shall be clean; wash me, and I shall be whiter than snow" (Psalm 51:7). David knows His God. He knows, like a good Father, what we ask for, we will receive. If you're feeling behind and covered up in dirt and stains, ask your Heavenly Father to remind you of what He has already done for you. The matter is settled.

"Lord, cleanse me."

43

HE MINISTERS TO US

One quiet evening, as the house settled down, I was sitting alone on the couch, about to join my husband in the room. I felt so overwhelmed and depleted that evening. We had an 8th-grade graduation and Senior Awards night after a long day of chemo for Mark. I could feel the pressure of the day pressing on my chest. I was just sitting in silence, breathing in and out, and a song popped into my head. "I need Thee. O, I need Thee. Every hour I need Thee." (Robert Lowry 1872). Then, as if Abba Himself swooped into the room, He filled my heart with one promise after another of all He does to minister to us, His children. "Cast all you care on him. For He cares for you" (1 Peter 5:7). "Come to me, all you who are weary and heavy laden, and I will give you rest" (Matthew 11:28). I heard Him whisper, "The Lord is close to the broken-hearted and saves those who are crushed in spirit. He protects all his bones, and not one of them is broken" (Psalm 34:18-19). And also, "He heals the brokenhearted and binds up all their wounds" (Psalm 147:3). These verses clearly communicate how our Heavenly Father ministers to us. And they are all true. But at that moment, on my couch, in my circumstances, Abba Father came down from heaven, met me there, and ministered to my heart with His Word. I have noticed in grief that Abba is tender and attentive. Like a good shepherd, He tends to our needs and ministers to our hearts. I love to see the way He will do it.

Sometimes it's through a friend who thoughtfully put a card in the mail, shot out a quick but meaningful text, or picked up the phone with one purpose, to minister to a weary soul. Other times it is through total strangers quick with a compliment or welcoming smile. His Word comes to mind at just the right time, or you hear a scripture verse on the radio. But when He chooses to enter your situation, and His presence fills your car or living room, His ministering Spirit surrounds you. Your burden is lifted, even for the moment, and you know you are not in this alone.

That is what our Heavenly Father does for us in hardship. He is with us. Christ came down to this earth, wrapped in limited human flesh, and felt what we felt. Scripture tells us He is familiar with our struggles (Hebrews 4:15). He came to save us. He also came to be relatable to us. We have a Savior who died and rose again and one who is familiar with what pains us. He was tempted just as we are. He cried, got angry, and was tired. When you've been through something similar with someone, you can better minister to them. You know. You have been there. As a perfect Savior, He ministers to us from a place of familiarity. Let Him minister to you today.

"Lord, here's my aching heart."

44

HE KNOWS US

Imagine standing in a long line. You're tired and frustrated. Alone. Then someone calls your name. You turn around to see your old friend walking towards you. She's comfortable and familiar. You visit for a few minutes and get caught up on how the families are doing. She goes her separate way, and you are still in that same line. Nothing has changed. You're still waiting, tired, still in line. But doesn't your heart feel lighter? Just to be known brings a settling to your heart and mind. It lifts the spirits. It brings encouragement, even though they did nothing to get you out of that line or move you ahead. But still, you feel better. It's not as tedious as it was. You smile, thinking how nice it was to know and be known as you wait.

Sometimes in this life, we have times of frustration. We're tired, exhausted even. And we can sure feel alone. I have been there. Watching Mark struggle physically gave me a sense of all those feelings; frustrated, tired, and even alone. I wanted so badly to help him not be sick, or at least not in so much pain. I wanted to make things easier for him. When I couldn't, I felt like I was alone in this battle to ward off all the side effects his body was processing. I cried out to God. I prayed in panic. Then, in the quiet, Abba would press in. My mind would go to all of the promises in His Word. They were familiar to me as I meditated on them. I began to be comforted by His truths.

God knows me. Jeremiah 1:5 boldly tells us, "Before I formed you in the womb I knew you…" Another truth in Luke 12:7 swept into my spirit and brought with it a renewed comfort: "Why, even the hairs on your head are numbered. Fear not, you are of more value than many sparrows." Nothing changed. I still sat beside Mark, longing to give him ease. But with this verse, I remembered that Abba Father knows me.

With our Heavenly Father, not only does He know us, but He is working in our circumstances for good. Such a random thought that He knows the number of hairs on my head, and yet, if He knows that, then He knows the longings of my heart. He knows what I cannot do.

He knows what needs to be done for me and my loved one. And we are not forgotten. He knows us. He is with us. He is working His good plan for us, even as we wait. Remember that He knows you when you feel forgotten, tired, and even frustrated. He loves you. He is working out the best plan for you.

"Father, Thank You for knowing me."

45

HE FORMS US

Genesis 1 is the beginning of all things. We read several times in the story that He spoke, and it was so. He spoke of the separation between land and sky. He spoke the sun, moon, and stars into place. Vegetation, plants, land animals, birds. All spoken into existence. Then He made man in His own image, after His likeness. And we see something that always amazes me in Psalm 139 in regards to this making of man: "For you formed my inward parts; you knitted me together in my mother's womb" (vs.13). Can you hear the difference? The other things were spoken with all authority and through His good will. Absolutely. But with man, He knitted us together. He formed our parts. Like an artist weighing each stroke of the brush. With care and concern for every detail, He didn't just speak, He got involved. With His own hands, He shaped and molded us into being. With such love and intentionality, we were crafted together by our Heavenly Father.

This truth penetrated my hurting heart one day as I sat in my sunroom, feeling forgotten in yet another battle that had come our way. I wondered if maybe God looked away for just a second and returned to see us spiraling downward, with the weight of the world crushing us. The call simply said, "It's in the lungs." We were always okay as long as it didn't spread to the lungs. And now, here we were. I sat in silence. My mind and heart straining to wrap around this raw news. I felt small and invisible. Then I saw a bird crafting its nest. I watched as it dropped to the floor of the forest, selectively chose a branch, then returned and wove that branch into its nest, carefully and intentionally. I began to think of the One who formed that bird, that tree—my husband's lungs. The One who created Mark's lungs was well aware of what was happening inside them. And it mattered to Him. I sat still and quiet in the presence of our Maker and cried. I held my hands up to Him and cried harder. I could not see beyond this horrible moment. But knowing the truth about our Lord, that He knit Mark's lungs together with such beauty and care, covered me in a peace that is beyond human understanding. And I surrendered Mark's lungs and my fragile heart to Him.

Because He formed us in our mothers' wombs, we can rest in Him. We can trust that even when things go wrong, He cares. He is with us. He has a plan for us. Knowing He loves us and is with us changes everything. Our outcome is in His hands, just as our unformed bodies began. When you feel invisible or buried under the weight of the world, remember that He formed your unseen body with His perfect love. Let Him form your broken heart again.

"Lord, I lay in Your arms. Form me."

46

HE SETTLES US

" And after you have suffered a little while...." (1 Peter 5:10). These words replayed in my mind one day after Mark had passed away. I reeled from all the suffering my husband endured. It chilled my bones to recount the effects of chemo or think about Mark's heart-wrenching question, "How do we tell the kids, Tina?" I couldn't make his suffering fit into the "little while" category. In grief, it's hard to see the whole picture, or in this case, the whole verse. We get stuck on the suffering part and can't get past it. Hope filled me as I willed my eyes to move to the rest of this verse. "...the God of grace, who has called you to his eternal glory in Christ, will *Himself* restore, confirm, strengthen, and establish you" (1 Peter 5:10, emphasis mine). Redemptive work is done by God Himself. He doesn't send an angel or just speak this into existence. He comes down and does this reparative work for us.

Psalm 103:14 reminds us that God is aware of our frailty. He knows our need to be rescued. And in His perfect time, He removes us from the heartaches of this world. Not too late or too early, but right on time. Through our battle, I questioned this with Abba more than once. I begged God to lighten Mark's load. I wanted peace in his mind and body. Yet, God was using Mark and his suffering for His glory. I saw Him reaching others through my husband's testimony and in his softened heart. Abba Father guided Mark into a closer walk with Him. And Mark surrendered more and more to His will for us. It humbled me. It brought me closer to my Father. It was a perfect example of what God does for us in our suffering and grief. If we allow Him, He softens our hearts, drawing us into a closer walk with Him while at the same time using our suffering to reach others in their place of frailty.

After Mark had gone Home to glory, I was able to go to Israel. I walked the Via Dolorosa, Christ's path of suffering to the Cross. If you didn't know, it is a long, winding, uphill, broken road—roughly 2,000 steps of difficult rocky ground. I walked it with a cold bottle of water in my hand. Still, I felt the weight of this procession to Christ's sacrifice. I envisioned the crowds staring, jeering, cursing, pushing, and hurling insults at Jesus as He walked this path. The humiliation, shame, and false accusations they spit at Him as He carried my cross on His back. I was undone when we got to the Place of the Skull. The sheer amount of pain and suffering He endured for me. Innocent of any sin, He suffered so profoundly for me.

At that moment, I thought of our "light and momentary sufferings" and thought of Paul's words that they are "incomparable to the glory that awaits" (Romans 8:18), and it hit me. We have not suffered to this point. When we are covered in real, daunting struggles, let's consider what Christ endured for us and focus on His plan to redeem each struggle, and each hardship we walk through, all for His glory in His time. I've experienced God setting up divine appointments for me to speak into a person's hurt, with an understanding that only comes from walking the hard road of sorrow, and have poured the truth of a redeeming Savior into their aching heart. He uses all of our suffering, giving it purpose and allowing us to share His healing through each encounter.

"O Lord, Thank You for Your plan of redemption."

47

HE CARRIES US

The decision was made. A reconstructed leg with a cadaver bone and what Mark called affectionately an erector set had to go. The cancer had returned in the same leg, in the same spot. We would amputate below the knee, remove the tumor, and pray it would remove the threat. Mark's outlook never ceased to amaze me. He was ready to get rid of the cancer and move on with his life. I, however, was not ready for any of it. I felt as if my own legs were failing me. I could not keep up with all our treatments and surgeries. And I felt as if I could not take my next step. How was Mark doing this? Isaiah 46:4b holds a precious truth from your Father above: "I have made you, and I will carry you; I will sustain you, and I will rescue you."

Isaiah 63:9 gives us a peek into the heart of God, as He feels with us in times of distress. "In all their affliction he was afflicted, and the angel of His presence saved them; in His love and in His pity he redeemed them; he lifted them up and carried them all the days of old." I have read this verse one hundred times. I believed it. But at this moment, when I thought I could not walk under the weight of this upcoming amputation, I had to believe it.

Sometimes in life, we get to live out what we believe. When we get the news. We hear the plan. But the plan is what we are afraid of. In these times, we can doubt and shrivel up in our faith, or we can see it as an opportunity to live out what we say we believe. He is either the God He claims to be or He is not. His word is either true and has saving power, or it does not. Have you ever been there? What we know of God's word is healing and words to live by, for sure. But these moments where we will either believe and live or indulge our disbelief and suffocate are defining moments for us. But who is doing the defining? God tells us He is with us and carries us when we can't carry ourselves through a struggle that paralyzes us. Isaiah 46:4b declares again, "... I am he who will sustain you. I have made you, and I will carry you; I will sustain you, and I will rescue you." He tells us He will never leave nor forsake us. And again, Isaiah 40:31 promises us this: "But they that wait for the Lord shall renew their strength; they shall mount up on wings as eagles; they shall run and not grow weary; they shall walk and not grow faint."

In times when we feel we cannot go on, our Heavenly Father carries us. He comes alongside us, holds us up, and carries us without hesitation. And not based on our own strength or ability. He carries us because He made us. We are His. When you feel like you can't take another step, just know that He carries us.

Give in to His grip, and rest in His arms. Sit quietly in His presence with the intent to absorb His unconditional love into your mind and spirit. Let your thoughts go to His promise to love you with everlasting love. Journal about how He shows you His love through those around you, the beauty and consistency of His nature out your window, or in bringing to your mind memories of how He cares for you. Soak up His love by carving out even a few moments of being intentionally present with your Lord today.

"Lord, carry me."

48

HE INVITES US

Scripture holds powerful truths about how we work and what's required for us to be effective, productive, refreshed, and refueled. In hardship, we desperately need to be replenished, sometimes moment by moment. Great news! Christ offers this to us. John 15:4 says, "Abide in Me, and I in you. As the branch cannot bear fruit by itself unless it abides in the vine, neither can you unless you abide in me." This does not mean to have an occasional encounter with our God, but to dwell with Him constantly. It's a declaration of how our strength and effectiveness work. We can not do without Him. When things are going smoothly, and all's right with the world, we cannot, and when we are in chaos and hardship, we cannot either. Our circumstances don't actually affect this truth. Apart from Him, we can do nothing (John 15:5b). We are so tired of grief that we think we are not measuring up. The truth? We weren't measuring up before our hardship hit. We can't. God knew this from the beginning. He offers this invitation. Remain in Me.

In Mark 1:17, He invites us to "Follow Me, and I will make you become fishers of men." The opportunity to produce spiritually and to contribute to the well-being of others is still on the table. Yes, even when we are suffering. Engaging in the betterment of others shifts our thinking from self to others. Remember how rewarding it is to be in the life-changing work of God. He includes us in His ministry when we come to Him and heed his invitation. This call to action lifts our spirits and gives us a bigger picture. Even in struggle, we can bless others.

There were many opportunities to serve others while we were in the throes of battling cancer. Mark took them. Honestly, at times he would drag me with him. But without fail, in our obedience, we were used to bless others. And we were always amazed at Abba's goodness to others and how it blessed us. Not only that but for that moment, we were soaking in God's kindness and goodness and free from our own hardship. Heading His invitations reminds us that God is good and we can receive His goodness even in our sorrow. When you feel lost in your hardship, consider looking up, and responding to His constant invitation to come, be filled, and be used for His glory. It will change your outlook and pump a good dose of energy into your soul.

"Lord, I accept Your invitation."

49

HE CREATES US

Genesis 1 accounts for Creation and how God made everything, including us. I love that our beginnings are recorded in His Holy Word. I love how this shapes our image. We are made in His likeness. He called us "very good". Eve was created specifically as a helper, and the treasure and value God places on our role as such in everyday life is beautiful. With all the years of hardship we had already faced up to this point in our journey with a cancer diagnosis, I was getting lost in who I was and what my role was, designed by Abba from the beginning. Hardship has a way of clouding our view of self. I needed clarity. I found a need to dive deeper into the depths of the hardship we were walking in, to see it through Christ's eyes, and try to make sense of how our sorrow fits into who we are and what God's plan for us truly is. I needed to see that I was who Christ says I am even in my hardship. I needed more to anchor my identity on. I felt like I was losing who I was with each battle, each setback, and each trauma we faced. Colossians 1:16 took me deeper into this beginning of myself: "For by Him, all things were created, in heaven and on earth, visible and invisible, whether thrones or dominions or rulers or authorities- all things were created through Him and for Him." Beyond the deep sleep and surgical removal of one rib, as God took from man to create woman (Genesis 2:21), I needed to know why. Why was I created? In the thick of hardship, I needed to know this. This verse tells me clearly why. For Him. I was created for my God.

I also needed to clarify how. "For you formed my inward parts; you knit me together in my mother's womb" (Psalm 139:13). The "how" positions God in respect to me. He was in the deepest, darkest part. He was orchestrating the very start of me. And with His own hands. He knit me together.

My next need was to know if His creation ended with the forming of my body. And, of course, scripture has the answer to that as well. Ephesians 2:10 declares, "For we are his workmanship, created in Christ Jesus for good works, which he prepared beforehand, that we should walk in them." So, this takes us to today. The now. Our current situation.

Yes, in the beginning, He created. Yes, it was done intimately by Him. Yes, for His purposes. But also, this act of God is continuing to create us. As His children, we are His workmanship. He created us to do good works for Him beyond our beginnings. He is currently creating in us clean hands and a right spirit (Psalm 51:10). This did not just occur at the beginning of time or at the beginning of our time. He is still creating us for His glory and purpose in the middle of our struggle.

I reached a point in my hardship, watching Mark and the kids struggle, where I wondered if God even saw us. If He even knew what was happening all around us and to us. Have you been there? In that place where you lost your way? Your purpose? Do you wonder if you are significant or even seen anymore? Jeremiah 1:5 brings to light the truth about us amid our struggles. "Before I formed you in the womb, I knew you, and before you were born, I consecrated you; I appointed you..." If you've forgotten who you are, go to His Holy Scriptures. Dive into the truth of what He says about you. See Him creating you through it all.

"Lord, create in me..."

50

HE ADORNS US

Adorn means adding something to make it more beautiful. We see God adorning His people with His glory in Ezekiel 16. In verse 8, God declares to the nation of Israel that He made them his own. He claimed these people for himself. Now, if you read this chapter, you may question the beauty it tells. It's titled: The Lord's Faithless Bride. But please stay with me. God reveals his chosen people. Period. They were rejected and outcasts. Yet God saw them, chose them, and claimed them as his own. He recalls to the reader that He "adorned [them] with ornaments and put bracelets on [their] wrists and a chain on [their] neck" (vs.11). He stepped into mankind's lack and lavished them. He made them beautiful. He added His seal of ownership to them and covered them in His beauty. He does the same for us. The rest of the chapter tells a horrid story of how His people rejected God's generosity and turned away from Him. If we keep reading, we see this happen again and again. I've always marveled at the unconditional love of our Lord and Savior. He knew the hearts of these people, yet He chose them once and for all. But this chapter is not about Israel's choices. It's about the character and choice of God, the Father.

I was going back through my journal some time ago, remembering the raw emotions of battling cancer with Mark and all my family endured during that decade of hardship. I saw the unrest, poor coping skills, and downright bad decisions we made during that time. My therapist says that happens when people are in distress. It certainly happened to the Israelites. We are not much different. And God sees us the same as He did the Israelites. And just as He did for the Israelites, He does with us. He adorns us. Nowhere in the Old Testament does it put any conditions on this lavish love of our Abba Father.

We can certainly see the flaws of these chosen people. We can see our flaws as well. The enemy would have us think we will lose God's favor if we don't handle difficulties in an honorable way. But this story shows us the faithful love of our Father and how it is not dependent on us. He adorns us. I have since learned that the wrong choices and poor character we sometimes display in hardship actually bring Him glory. His steadfast love is evident in our marred stories. His faithfulness shines through in our weakness. He loves us purely and without condition, regardless of our faithlessness. Regardless of ourselves. He is glorified in our hardship and ugliness. He takes our ugly and turns it into beauty. His response to us, even in our failures, is to adorn us. When we fail Him, He makes us beautiful. If you're struggling with choices made in hardship that mar your view of yourself, let God adorn you with His beauty.

"Lord, make me beautiful."

III. WHAT HE SAYS

There is a self-narrative every human soul knows. In hardship, we are our own worst critic. It's been said we are our own worst enemy. Knowing what God says about us in hardship changes how we see our situation. It changes how we see hope and healing for ourselves and those around us who are in the struggle with us. His narrative of us is full of grace and mercy. It is centered on the truth of ourselves and our circumstances. When we know what He says about us, we can let go of our self-narrative and tune into His, which is full of truth, grace, and mercy. In this place, we heal. We must know what our Heavenly Father says about us to get through hardship.

51

"BEGIN."

Have you ever stopped and thought about the Beginning? Sure, we've read the story in Genesis of how God made everything, but when was the last time you thought about this truth and what it means to us? Genesis says, "In the beginning…" God, the creator of time and all things, started life. He began it. The author of all life, the Creator of all living things, started our world. Reading through this account of the beginning in Genesis chapter 1, you get a clearer picture of our Father, His plan, and His heart. It starts with a fascinating display of authority, amazement, awe, and wonder, and that's just the first day! We see the unfolding of this beautiful world and all the creatures He saw fit to place here. The intricate details of a God of order, generosity, and wisdom. Every detail is so specific our brains cannot fathom them all. He looks back on every day of creation, assesses His work, and declares it "good." Then, on the last day, He created the most extraordinary, highly regarded creation, man. We know this because we are the only created thing He gave His image to. We are made in His likeness and are given purpose, meaning, work, and relationship.

God wanted a relationship with us. He began all of life and created a world to place us in. Then He gave us each other to learn how to love Him, by loving one another. Finally, He gave us His Presence. He looked back at us and declared, "Very good." He spoke everything we would need into existence, and then He marveled at His work. Why does this matter in our hardship? This account not only shows us our worth to the Creator of all things but tells us that one day it won't be like this. One day, when He returns and takes us to His home, all of this will be changed. We will be with Him, face to face, and He will begin again, but with new bodies, unveiled minds, and no distance between our Creator

Savior God and us! The proclamation to begin tells us there is more. There is a middle, and there will be an end. Revelation tells us there will be another beginning! In a new world, with a new Heaven, in our new bodies! When God began life, He knew then we would need a Savior, He would come and save us, and we would one day be reunited face-to-face with the One whose image we bear! Oh, let your mind meditate on this truth!

Whatever you face, because it has a beginning, will end. And one day, as we begin our eternity, as promised, and will be in paradise with our Lord and Savior. Let this truth change how we view our current situation, and rejoice in the heart of our Father and His good plan!

"Father, Thank You for Your good plan!"

52

"I'VE GOT THIS."

I love that we have a track record of God's relationship with mankind. Starting in Genesis, the beginning of man, extending to the beginnings of The Church, and completing this world in all of His promises in Revelation. God's Word is overflowing with evidence of His faithfulness and ability to care for, rescue, heal, and help us through this life. We see His steadfast love repeatedly extended, even in our faithlessness. The Psalmist reminds us in Psalm 139 that God knits us together in our mother's womb. He saw our unformed bodies. He knows us. This means He knows our inabilities, imperfections, and intentions as well. He knows what we lack and need, even before we ask. He knows what we are capable of and what we are not. He knew at the beginning we would need a Savior. That's always been part of His plan.

I also love that God knows every detail about us. He knows we lean on self-reliance, think too highly of ourselves, and often find ourselves in over our heads. This world is too much for us. Sin has created a heaviness our feeble minds and bodies can't seem to hold up under. What is His response to our inability? He holds our face gently in His hands and declares, "I've got this." Scripture is filled with reminders of God's ability to hold us, grow us, rescue us, and be our rock and refuge. 2 Corinthians 9:8 tells us His response to our insufficiency: "And God is able to make all grace abound to you, so that having all sufficiency in all things at all times, you may abound in every good work." How do we receive what we need? His grace is freely extended to those who are His own. We see in 2 Timothy 1:12 that when we focus on Christ, we can be assured that God will guard what He has entrusted to each of us until He returns. Our life is in His hands. We cannot fail! Acts 20:32 reminds us that God can build us up and provide what we need in whatever we go through.

Philippians 3:21 proclaims that everything on this earth is subjected to the power of Jesus. Therefore, we can boldly rest in knowing that He's got this! We can rest in Him, be lifted up by Him, be satisfied in Him, and be guarded by Him. In this life, we will have trouble (John 16:33), but take heart. He's got this!

"Lord, Thank You for having me in this crazy life."

53

"I'M NOT LEAVING."

Have you ever felt abandoned? How about like you've lifted your head up to find no one near you, no one to help? Going through hardship can feel like there is no one close enough who understands or is willing to walk this uphill battle with you. I've been there. It's lonely. It feels like the best thing to do is to embrace the isolation since it feels inevitable. But there is a friend who is closer than a brother (Proverbs 18:24). This truth seems best understood when we are in hardship. I have found that when life is loneliest, His presence and promise never to leave us nor forsake us are easiest to receive and understand (Deuteronomy 31:8). The enemy uses isolation and lies to get us to give up our hope and decrease our faith in our Lord and Savior. And when we face hardship, we are most vulnerable to these tactics.

I grasped God's word in my darkest hours one night as I felt the world leave me. Already feeling isolated from all the hardship we had endured, more was coming. In these next few days, I felt the amount of people who could understand all I was feeling grow smaller and smaller. I felt myself sinking into a crack where no one could reach me. We had just learned that we had to amputate Mark's leg above the knee. We had already lost his limb below the knee. And now more would be lost. This meant gait training and for my husband to learn a new way of walking. What would that look like? How was Mark going to approach this new challenge? How would I feel through all of this learning, trying, and frustration? I could already feel the lonely setting in. Who would understand what we were going through? Who could we go to when we had questions or needed advice on how to deal with these unique issues related to above-the-knee amputation? We did not know anyone else who had gone through this. Loneliness was creeping into our minds as we faced this unknown.

In this time of true isolation and fear that we were falling into a hole of the unknown, I was reminded that my God has no limits to His understanding. Can He comprehend the kind of loss that is so personal? Does He know what being ripped apart feels like? Is He able to tune into our greatest fear and cover us with a personal, intimate knowing of our pain and what we need most? Yes. He is the Creator of all and our personal Friend. Psalm 147:5 simplified my grave concern and soothed my fear of falling beyond His grasp with this simple truth about our Lord and Savior. "His understanding is infinite." The One who made Mark's leg, and our souls, can infinitely understand all we feel, see, hear, endure. And He is enough. Knowing this puts our minds at ease. We didn't have all the answers. We didn't have any. But our God would be with us every step of the way. He would provide all we needed and be our comfort in the meantime. That truth blew the winds of uncertainty away, and both my husband and I were able to take a breath and declare with confidence, "What then shall we say? If God is for us, who can be against us?" (Romans 8:31). This was our truth, and it is yours too, even today in your hardship. When loneliness comes calling, be at ease.

"Lord, You don't leave me lonely."

54

"I'LL COME TO YOU."

L uke tells a story of a lost sheep. Even though I was trying to cling to my Savior in our difficulties, my grief seemed to be driving me away from Him. In hardship, sometimes we can relate to the one sheep who has strayed from the fold. But really, straying from our Shepherd paints an image of every human soul. At some point in our lives, we recognize that we have strayed, or are straying from our Good Shepherd, and we feel far from His saving grip. Sometimes our wandering from His side isn't an intentional act of rebellion. In our sorrow, our eyes are taken off of Him and onto pain. Our grief becomes the focus and our emotions drive us away from His side. So what does scripture tell us He does when one has strayed from Him? He leaves the ninety-nine (Luke 15:4-7). Hardship has a way of making us feel unreachable. Yet, even in hardship, He goes with us. He remains. He does not leave us. Have you ever felt lost? Ever been in a place where you didn't think anyone could find you? Hidden from the rest of the world?

I remember when Mark and I had been arguing about the pain medicine his doctor wanted to give him. These drugs were so powerful they scared me. These drugs were made specifically for patients with cancer in their bones. Excruciating. But still, I was terrified. We argued and could not come to a common ground. And I felt like no one understood what we were going through. They certainly could not understand my opinion. After all, my body was not experiencing this horrific pain. Even close friends said, "Tina, let him decide." They were right, but I felt unheard, unseen, and hidden from the rest of the world at that moment. Mark did too. He didn't know the answer. The pain meds scared him too. We both felt like we were on some lone island, but not even together.

God's word swooped in and met us in this lonely, confusing place.

There was no place we could go where God would not be there with us. Our battle with cancer and all the ripple effects that accompanied highlighted the truth of His omnipresence. No hardship or trouble we face on this earth can separate us from His love. Knowing this brought Mark and I back together, on the same page, and created solid ground for us to face the darkness. We had Christ drawing us to His side and together. God, in his unending mercy and perfect love, goes with us. To places we never expected to go and have no idea how to get out of.

When we can't find our way out, much less find our way to Him, He says, "I'll come to you." He is not like any other authority in our lives. There are no conditions. No limits to where He goes with us. Nothing we find ourselves walking through surprises Him. And He is not bothered, frustrated, or put out by our inability to get to Him. He is familiar with all of our shortcomings. He chooses to show up again and again and love us. Always. That is who He is. It's His nature. So if you find yourself in a place you can't get out of, if you can't get to God, He will come to you. Always.

"O Lord, find me."

55

"THIS WAY."

One ominous morning we struggled to find the correct place to park at the hospital our doctors referred us to. Duke is a massive facility, and we felt lost. Once we entered the hospital, there was a Help Desk with smiling faces, ready and able to tell us how to get to where we needed to be. It was a relief to get questions answered and some direction on that scary day.

God helps us in our time of need. We see God's guidance throughout the scriptures, from the Old Testament to the New. As a people prone to wander, He knows we need direction. His word provides that. His Holy Spirit does, too. God tells us through David, "I will instruct you and teach you in the way you should go; I will counsel you with my eye upon you" (Psalm 32:8). What a promise in our hardship. With His eye upon us, He shows us the way. In our case above, it was through the kind hearts working the Help Desk in Duke that day. Other times, a neighbor. Or, alone in our living room, with an open Bible in our lap. Through a timely sermon or just in bringing to our memory His word, hidden in our hearts.

One of my favorite verses is Isaiah 30:21, "And your ears shall hear a word behind you, saying, 'This is the way, walk in it,' when you turn to the right or when you turn to the left." If you start at the beginning of this chapter in Isaiah, you catch a glimpse of where these words fit into the story of the world. The Israelites are being told the truth about themselves. They are rebellious. They lack. They are in defiance of their Creator God. And God's response? This section begins in verse 18 and is subtitled simply, "The Lord Will Be Gracious." He lists the ways they are rebelling. He shows them the true condition of their hearts. Then He shows them the way through His own heart. He extends His grace. What a Savior.

In my journey through the grief of losing Mark, at times, it has felt as if I was distant from my Savior. It became too heavy. I came to the end of my ability and hope. God's response? He has been gracious to me. As He shows me again and again in His word, and as He uses others He has placed in my life to speak encouragement into me, His grace becomes the clear path for my next step. The Israelites continued to turn from the Lord. They continued to get lost. But the Lord shows us through them that their ability and their faith are not a factor in His faithfulness to show us the way. He shows us the way despite our broken condition. Psalm 91:15 promises, "When he calls to me, I will answer him; I will be with him in trouble; I will rescue him and honor him." He doesn't stop showing us the way. He walks us home. He honors us. Do you feel like your circumstances have made you wander from His side? Just hold on. He has spoken, and He will do it.

"Lord, show me the way."

56

"YOU ARE FORGIVEN."

"I forgive you." How healing is this statement, offered in mercy and love? God is a forgiving God, responding to all who call to Him (Psalm 86:5). His word tells us this. His history with mankind reveals this. 2 Corinthians covers this truth in greater detail: "All this is from God, who reconciled us to himself through Christ and gave us the ministry of reconciliation; that God was reconciling the world to himself in Christ, not counting people's sin against them..." He declares us forgiven and reconciled with God through the blood of Jesus. Colossians paints the picture of why this is a necessary gift. "Once you were alienated from God and were enemies in your minds because of your evil behavior. But now he has reconciled you by Christ's physical body through death to present you holy in his sight, without blemish and free from accusation..." (Colossians 1:21-22). These verses clarify our need for a Savior and God, and that need is met through his Son, Jesus Christ. We are forgiven. 1 John 1:9-10 tells us, "If we confess our sins, he is faithful and just to forgive us our sins and to cleanse us from all unrighteousness." It is that simple.

In turbulent times in our lives, things get complicated quickly. This truth remains. You see, it is not dependent on our circumstances. If we confess, He is faithful. Simple. In the middle of our crazy battle with cancer, nothing was simple, reliable, or right. Our whole world seemed chaotic and unpredictable. We never knew what the chemo would do to his body or when/where the cancer would return. We could not have predicted how our children would cope with this devastation. But one thing never changed. God's forgiveness remained. The work Christ completed on the cross never ceased or changed or was watered down. Our rock-solid foundation remained. Our circumstances faltered. Our faith did too. And He forgave us. The rest of 2 Corinthians came to life for us: "And he has committed to us the message of reconciliation. We are, therefore, Christ's ambassadors, as though God were making his appeal through us" (2 Corinthians). During our battle, God's faithful promises rang true. And those around us saw His never-ending love remain. We became ambassadors for Christ. Through us, Christ's love and constant forgiveness came through. Not because of us. But His word and His promises faithfully stand.

In rare moments, God lets us be the billboard for His heart. Cling to His word and trust He is doing His good word in you, through you, for His glory, and those around you.

"Lord, You declare me forgiven."

57

"I ADORE YOU."

It had been an extra difficult day. Fresh out of Mark's surgery to amputate his left leg, it was 8th-grade graduation. Mark was determined to be there for our youngest son. I wanted to pass this one hard, hoping our son would understand. Mark was not hearing it. He was pale, weak, and racked with pain, but he was attending his son's graduation. Period. I was exhausted, reeling in a state of shock. Wanting to dig my heels in and refuse to go anywhere. But instead, I sighed loudly and said, "Okay. We'll go." Mark quietly said these words and my whole world shifted. "I adore you." Oxford's definition of adore is to love and respect someone deeply. But how could Mark adore me?

At that moment, I was showing my true heart; stubborn, tired, and angry. He melted my attitude with this one declaration. I didn't deserve for my husband to adore me. I was not on board with his larger-than-life determination to be present for our son's big night. I only gave in because I was too numb to argue. Yet, Mark adored me.

I have come to realize that my actions did not earn his adoration. It was a decision Mark made. I was not hiding my true heart in that conversation. He saw it. The anger. The self-indulgence. At that moment, I was not adorable. Yet he chose to adore me. It was not a hard stretch to equate Mark's decision to declare me adorable with Abba Father's decision to adore me as well. His love far exceeds any earning we could attempt on our own. We can't earn it. We aren't that great, actually. And so many times when we are in hardship, it's the worst that comes out, not the best. Yet God tells us in His word that He adores us. He chooses to love us deeply. Not because of our feelings, actions, or attitudes. He adores us because of who He is. And that never changes, regardless of our situation, attitude, or feelings. God is our Good Father. Our Shepherd.

Our Comforter. Zechariah 2:8 calls us the apple of His eye. That means we are simply the reflection in His eye, which is only possible because He is close to us, gazing at us, adoring us. Scriptures say His thoughts towards us are good and too many to count (Psalm 139:17). John 3:16 states clearly, "For God so loved the world that he gave his only son…" while we were still sinning (Romans 5:8).

I needed to hear that on that horrible day, and maybe you need to hear it now. Today, take time to quiet your heart. Close your eyes, soak up these verses of truth, and let God adore you. Yes, in your mess, bad attitude, or self-indulgence. He adores you. It's who He is.

"Lord, Thank You for who You are."

58

"I'VE GOT A GOOD PLAN."

What can a plan do for us? Mark always had a plan. It kept him focused, determined, accountable, and crystal clear on what was next. I loved how effortlessly he led our family. He would say, "Without a plan, you're spinning in circles." I'd love to argue, but my personality tested that theory too often. I'm a bit of a fly-by-the-seat-of-your-pants gal. I made myself motion sick with all the spinning I did. Humbly, I agree. Having a plan is a good thing. Know who else has a plan? God does.

He tells us plainly in Jeremiah 29:11 that He knows the plans He has for us. Good plans. Plans to help and not harm us. Plans to give us a future and a hope. Plans give us a vision for the task at hand. Scripture shows that without a vision, the people perish (Proverbs 19:18). In the hardest parts of our battle, I felt as if we were perishing. Spinning. Without a plan. But the truth was that God did have a plan even when we couldn't see it.

We don't always understand His plans for us and it's hard to accept something we don't understand, but the good news is we don't have to understand to trust Him. We have the history of mankind to lean on. From the first man, we see God's clear, good plan, which includes us thousands of years after life began. In Revelation, we get a sneak peek into the end of God's good plan where He takes us to Heaven to live with Him for eternity where there is no more sickness, tears, separation, sorrow, or want. As hard as it is to accept, our sufferings on this earth are part of this plan. He promises to take our sufferings and turn them into good (Romans 8:28). He promises to right all the wrongs in His time (Ecclesiastes 12:14). In hard times, the enemy wants us to turn on God, abandon our faith, and spin out of control. As in the Garden, Satan attempts to trip us up by twisting God's word so we will doubt God and hide from Him. But God has a plan. He is with us even when we can't see any evidence of this. He strengthens us with his right hand, in the midst of our greatest weakness. He puts an end to our suffering one day (Isaiah 41:10).

That day is coming. We can trust Him. We can trust His plan. When life wraps its hand around your neck and tries to squeeze the breath out of you, hold fast to God's promises. Trust His plan, even if you can't understand it. And know that He is in control, bringing us to a place where all is redeemed. Let your troubles here on earth point your heart toward Him and His good plan. He is able, and He will do it.

"O Lord, help me to trust Your plan."

59

"WORSHIP ME."

God's word is full of calls to worship Him. When. Where. How and why. For some, worship comes naturally. Others are more reserved. Sometimes, worship flows freely from our lips; other times, it feels fake and forced. Yet, He calls us to do this act of humbling ourselves and focusing on Him. Where does this fit in our suffering? What if we're too broken? Too distracted by our circumstances? What then? He still calls us to worship Him. So, how do we do this in hardship?

Psalm 100 is pretty clear on the how. "Make a joyful noise unto the Lord. Serve the Lord with gladness; come into his presence with singing!" (vs.1-2). Seems like a contradiction to our circumstances at times. But if we continue reading this psalm, we better understand why and how to do this in our struggle: "Know that the Lord is God. It is he who made us, and we are his; we are his people, the sheep of his pasture" (vs3). How can we worship joyfully in our grief? Because we are His. He knows us and our circumstances. He is our Shepherd and Creator. He knows what we need and has the resources to provide for our lack.

The next verse tells us how to do this even in sorrow. "Enter his gates with thanksgiving and his courts with praise; give thanks to him and praise him." I know this may be one of the hardest things to do when we are down. So why does He expect us to have this joyful heart in trials? It is what carries us out of it. He knows that staying in our sorrow, eyes clouded with grief, and a one-track focus on self does not serve us. It does not help us in our time of need. Setting our minds on Him does.

Choosing thanksgiving and praise when it hurts refocuses us on truth. It breeds hope. It changes our viewpoint. It ushers in life and healing. The Giver of Life knows us. When we worship Him, we get lost in His truth. One Sunday, I was sitting in church, honestly in body only. My mind was wondering what the next week held for us. I looked over and saw my husband and daughter doing that barely-in-control shoulder shake, about to burst into uncontrollable laughter in the middle of the service and interrupt the message for that day. I tried the scolding look, but that only made them shake harder. I had to look away. Later, as we were leaving, our pastor came up to them and, with a grin from ear to ear, said, "I'd love to know what was so funny." They burst into laughter and said something the preacher said gave them both an image of God dancing around His throne under a disco ball. Now all three were dying laughing, and I had to give in to the joy.

Joy amid hardship gives us the grace and ability to relax and laugh in the midst of turmoil. Letting God come into our hard situation and breathe a respite right in the middle of a sermon, because He is with us, knows us, and provides for us, affords us a moment to let down our guard and laugh. We can worship Him when we trust His plan and heart for us.

"Lord, help me to rejoice in You."

60

"YOU CAN TRUST ME."

So many stories in the Bible point to the ability to trust in a God we know, personally and intimately. Deborah is one of those stories that resonates with this truth; We can trust a God we know. In Judges, Deborah shows us the need to trust God and believe His words before we see them (Judges 4). She believed the victory was theirs even before the fight began. How could she trust God before it happened? She knew Him. She knew He knew her and that He was with her and her people. He called her as He still calls to us. "Trust me." The power of His testimony is recorded in the Bible. We see how He saves mankind again and again. He has built His trust by remaining faithful to His creation, and we can trust Him based on His history with mankind. But there is another way in which we can be assured of His faithfulness: by looking at our own track record with Him. As we walk in hardship we can see Him with us in many ways. We see His provision through those around us. We see His faithfulness in our next breath. It's truly His will that allows us to expand our lungs and be here to tell our story one more day. It's because of His faithfulness you are here, holding this book. Just look around you and you will see all He has faithfully provided for you. We know Him. We can trust Him. And if we know Him, we can trust Him to show up and provide even before we see any evidence that help is on its way.

Throughout the scriptures, we see opportunities for God's people to trust even in difficult circumstances. We also see the rewards of trusting Him in those times before we can see evidence of His help. Let's look at the Red Sea fiasco. Although the Israelites wavered, Moses did not. And the sea parted and made a way that was not there moments before. Moses trusted when they seemed to be hemmed in. And God showed up. He calls all of us to trust Him in this manner before we see the answer. Mark would say this about each hurdle we had to face: "Well, this is another opportunity we get to live out what we say we believe." And you know what? We would choose to trust God before the answer was there, and our faith grew. Every time. Is this hard? Yes. Is it scary? That, too. But does God deliver? Every time. Without exception. And in this faith walk, we grow in our belief in our good God. "Those who trust in God are like Mount Zion, which cannot be shaken, but endures forever" (Psalm 125:1 NIV).

This call to trust Him before we see His help comes with so many blessings. "But those who trust in the Lord will renew their strength; they will soar like eagles, they will run and not grow weary, they will walk and not faint" (Isaiah 40:31). Jeremiah 17:7-8 (NIV) tells us, "Blessed are those who trust in the Lord and have made the Lord their hope and confidence." Throughout the scriptures, we can easily see the benefits as He calls us to trust Him. As hard as it is in difficult times, lean into His word, rely on His promises, and trust Him. You will not be let down.

"Lord, even before I see Your hand, I trust in You."

61

"I AM FOR YOU."

"For behold, I am for you, and I will turn to you, and you will be cultivated and sown" Ezekiel 36:9. This verse in Ezekiel seems like it doesn't fit into this declaration God makes of us. He declares that He is for us. So, how is He for us as He cultivates and changes us? Let's look further into some definitions of the word "cultivate." Cultivate means to refine and educate. It also means to be polite and civilized, to foster and grow, and to improve by labor and care (Merriam-Webster). In hardship, we seldom think of growth. Instead, hardship paints a picture of staying stuck or drowning. It feels like injury more than growth, and we hardly feel useful.

Many times, I felt attacked by the hardship we faced as a family. No, not by human force, but spiritually. We woke up on guard, expecting more bad news. Many days, we got it. I remember feeling depleted before my feet even hit the floor to face the new day.

David was familiar with this defeated and attacked feeling as well. He wrote in Psalm 56:9, "Then my enemies will turn back in the day when I call; This I know, that God is for me." David was also familiar with God as his source of help. "The Lord is with me; I will not be afraid. What can mere mortals do to me?" (Psalm 118:6 NIV). For me and my family, God used the church to help us in our defeated times. He also used people from Mark's work. People we knew were also dealing with big things, yet still willing to come alongside us. This kind of help humbled us. Our church prepared meals for ten months straight while we battled for Mark's life. Ten months... what a blessing they were to us in our time of need. Mark's coworkers and their families sent cards of encouragement at just the right time and loved us through spontaneous acts of service.

Maybe you've seen this truth that God is for you, played out in your own life. Maybe you've received help as well in the form of your church family or neighbors reaching out through meal deliveries when your family has been in need. It's a powerful, humbling kind of help we all need yet wrestle to accept, regardless of how needy our reality is at some point. God, doing the work through others, keeps His promise to us, that He is for us. He is willing to send help and be the help of His people. Prompting those around us to be His hands, His feet, His lips speaking encouragement over us.

This is how God shows us He is for us. He is fighting this battle alongside us. Through His church, His people. Through His Holy Spirit. Sometimes, I felt His tender presence on the coldest of nights, dwelling in my living room or at my bedside. As Mark wrestled with breathing, I wrestled with my faith. Yet I remained. Mighty to save. "The Lord your God is living among you. He is a mighty Savior." Zephaniah 3:17a became a reality to us. Other times, as I ran to His word, frazzled in my faith, He met me there. He remained by our side in all the horrible and the struggle. He is for us. We lived this out in very raw moments.

This truth that God is on our side was taught to us through His church, His word, and His very presence. It was even His Spirit that prompted us to seek Him. And by His great grace, we did. This world presents so many other choices to run to in our time of need. Our own flesh even deceives and tries to distract us with temporary gratifications, and we tried these other options, but when we ran to Him, He met us. He wrapped His arms around us and was our ever-present help. Psalm 34:4 became my personal prayer, "I sought the Lord, and he answered me; he delivered me from all my fears.".

When you are there, in that place where there seems to be no help, look to Him. He is for you.

"I Am, fight for me."

62

"I NEVER SLEEP."

Sleep. A valuable commodity. A lost treasure in hardship. I am not sure how we got through some days, depleted of sleep. Long days of treatments, tests, runs to specialty doctors, worry, and strife were all culprits of stolen sleep that accompanied our journey. And sleep deprivation does bad things to the mind, body, and spirit. It can create all kinds of problems for the human body. Our immune system gets compromised. Our breathing and digestive systems, too. It's difficult for our minds to process when we are experiencing sleep deprivation. We are slower, foggier, and less able to reason without sleep. Lack of sleep can even cause depression. Yet, when we sleep, we are more vulnerable. We aren't using our senses to survey our area. Our guard is down in sleep. Our systems slow to a bare minimum so that what is needed most gets the focus and energy. We lock doors, shut off lights, and safeguard our homes as we get much-needed sleep every night. That's what we must do to replenish our sleep each night. We were built to reset each twenty-four-hour period in time. God made us this way. For us, sleep is a must. And when we don't have it, we suffer.

But God is not human. Scripture tells us that He does not sleep. So, why does that matter to us? We know God is not human. We know He is not created. Why is this truth so important to us? How does this truth help us in our time of need? We have a God who is not restricted to human needs. He needs nothing. And a Creator God who does not need anything can rescue, protect, guard, and stand in all power and authority over us as we sleep. God lacks nothing at all times. He is always complete. He doesn't even need to take a break, lock up the house, and rest. Psalm 121 reassures Israel that their God, the One True God, does not sleep, nor does He slumber. His promise to guard and protect them rings true. If you look at the entire psalm, you will see the clear message to the Israelites. Their help comes from the Lord, a God who will not let their foot slip. He is their keeper. He keeps them from evil. He keeps their comings and their goings. He never sleeps. They can rest easy under a God who is not human and needs nothing. A God who keeps His promises to them. He does the same for us today. We can trust God because He does not sleep.

God knows we need to rest. He knows we need to shut down and reset. In times of trouble, He is aware of our frailty and needs to be protected as we vulnerably refresh our minds, bodies, and spirits. He can protect and provide for us in our weakness. When you can't keep your eyes open one more minute, lay your head down and rest in this truth: God does not sleep.

"Lord, be my protection."

63

"LISTEN, I AM SPEAKING."

Evidence of God speaking to His people runs like a cord throughout Scripture. He speaks in the storm and the calm. He speaks at sunrise and sunset. He speaks in the desert and the promised land. He speaks to us. So, what is He saying to us in our hardship? I believe the answer lies in His Word and His history with mankind.

God is the same yesterday, today, and tomorrow (Hebrews 13:8). The God of Abraham, Isaac, and Jacob is the same as the God in the New Testament, as He established his church for both Jews and Gentiles. He is the same God that formed me in my mother's womb in 1970. And He is the same God who is right beside you, speaking His truth, His plan, His promises into your weary heart today. 1 Kings 19 holds a powerful example of God speaking to Elijah in hiding, terrified for his life. God calls him out of his hiding to speak to him. He sends powerful wind, rain, and fire. Yet, it's in the whisper Elijah hears God. Giving instruction. Speaking of Elijah's protection and his next assignment. When Elijah is paralyzed with fear, He helps Elijah move out of fear into action (1 King 19:1-21).

I remember a time when I was paralyzed with fear. The diagnosis was ominous. The outcome was grim. I felt the world caving around me and my faith being snuffed out. How can we walk this path of cancer with our faith intact? God held my hand, raised my head, and stood by me. It wasn't an instant gain, but over the next weeks, I began to see that it was God's strength coursing through both Mark and myself, enabling us to breathe, share, and rest in His presence.

I stand here today, writing this book, by His strength and because of His promises. He spoke to me words of encouragement and strength, just as He did Elijah. Just as He is speaking to you, friend. Mark 4 records the account of Jesus calming the sea. He issues the command to the waters, "Peace! Be still!" and the raging wind and waves dissipate. And the fear in the disciples dies down, too. Jesus speaks peace into the waters and the hearts of His frantic disciples. He does the same for us in our desperation. God speaks to us each morning of His faithfulness and steadfast love through each sunrise. Nature is a big way God speaks to us. The rustling leaves remind us of His presence always with us. The beautifully robed flowers of His provision for us. God also speaks to us through those He puts in our path, who love Him and are willing to come alongside us and be encouraging in our time of need. He speaks to us through His Word and even gives us His Holy Spirit to understand. He is always speaking to us.

God is always speaking to us. His words bring us life and rest, healing, and strength. Be still. Be quiet. Listen, He is speaking to you.

"Lord, I am listening."

64

"I VALUE YOU."

To value someone is to put great personal importance on them. Typically, we humans value what is beautiful, useful, or desirable. But God does not have the same standards. He does not look at the same things we look at. What matters to Him is different than what matters to us. So, does God really value us? And if so, why? And what does that mean to us? Let's look at Matthew 6. Christ is talking about the value He and His Father have placed on man. "Look at the birds of the air; they neither sow nor reap nor gather in barns, and yet your Heavenly Father feeds them. Are you not more valuable than them?"

Have you ever gone to a park or a backyard, sat down, and listened to the trees? My best friend has a sanctuary for a backyard. I find myself drawn to it any time I visit her. Hundreds of birds make their homes right in her backyard. I was sitting there one morning in July, hardly able to think, mesmerized by the sounds of these beautiful birds. Suddenly I found myself thrown into worship, amazed at this passage and this whole other world God tends to. Yet, we are more valuable than they are to our Creator God. He whispered to me and asked, "Tina, do you trust Me?" My spirit answered before I could think, "Yes, Lord! I do." Little did I know that later that day, on our drive home, we'd get the call that our oldest had overdosed and was unresponsive.

In that experience, God showed me how He values us. He calmed my heart when I faced the possibility of having to bury my child. He was right there, with my son, as his breath waned and his system was overloaded with drugs. He called us His own, and despite our decisions or actions, He loved us. The profound lesson for me on that day was that God did not put conditions on His value of us. He didn't scold me for forgetting Him in my sheer horror and panic. He didn't tell my son,

"Well, you did this to yourself, so save yourself." Our actions did not cause His value on us to waver. He treasured us in our mess. And He put a value on our life, broken and destitute as it was on that day. My son did get out of that hospital and lives today as a bilateral amputee, praising God and glorifying Him in his story. I still rush ahead of God and sometimes take Him out of the equation, causing unnecessary stress and strain. And God still values us and loves us perfectly. He still rescues us when things out of our control happen and when we dig a huge pit and fall into it. Again, in Matthew 10:28, He reiterates, "Fear not, therefore. You are of more value than many sparrows."

Still not grasping this truth? Romans 5:8 says, "God showed His love for us in that while we were yet sinners, Christ died for us." He values us. Not because we deserve it or can handle this world's strife with grace or grit. He values us because He chose to do so. It is who He is. We may not get the outcome we desire. I wish my son still had his legs. I wish I could stop doubting my Savior. But do you see the beauty in His value? It does not change.

He treasures us. Even when we are in the throes of tragedy. Even when we ignore Him and do damage to ourselves. He says we have worth and value. Sink into His arms and be valued.

"Lord, show me my worth."

65

"I'M NEAR YOU."

❝The Lord is close to the brokenhearted and saves those who are crushed in spirit" Psalm 34:18 (NIV). Words can hardly cover the sheer comfort this truth brings. Brokenhearted described most of our 8 ½ year battle with cancer. Some are brokenhearted by God when they face trials. I was brokenhearted for Mark, watching all he suffered through. It breaks our hearts to see our loved ones suffer. Even after my husband went Home, I wrestled with this ache whenever I thought of how he suffered. He was in pain with every step he took. He suffered through treatments and surgeries, which frankly broke my heart.

Have you ever been there? Not even blaming anyone. Just brokenhearted by this life. Loss does that to us. It can rattle our souls. It can alter our way of processing life. I have been there. It's dismal. Lonely. Dark. Yet, Abba Father tells us He draws near to us in these times. He doesn't watch from a distance. He doesn't wring his hands and worry. He draws near. He carries the burden of grief with us. He provides a sense of togetherness with Him, and the gift of fellow believers He brings to us in our time of need. He puts us in the hearts of willing servants who reach out through a text, phone call, or note in the mail. Do these tangible acts of nearness take away the suffering? Do they make it alright again? No. I wish they did. But what they do for us is enough in that moment.

He enters our pain and confusion. He enters our anger and misunderstanding. He isn't afraid of our emotions or questions. He welcomes them. He says, "Cast all your cares on me." Why? Because He cares for us (1 Peter 5:7). Again, we see in Psalm 23:4 (KJV), "Yea, though I walk through the valley of the shadow of death, I will fear no evil; for thou are with me; thy rod and thy staff they comfort me." On this earth, we walk through the valley of the shadow of death. We do. He knew we would. And He wants us to know that He goes there with us. He pulls us into Himself. He won't leave us or forsake us (Deuteronomy. 31:6). It's hard to know this because when we are in that valley, our emotions sometimes cloud everything around us. But remember, our emotions do not determine God's actions.

When we are in distress and call out to Him, there He is. He is our help and sustainer. Jeremiah writes, "I called on your name, O Lord, from the depths of the pit; you heard my plea, 'Do not close your ear to my cry for help!' You came near when I called on you; you said, 'Do not fear'" (Lamentations 3:55-57). He dispels fear and doubt when He draws near. We have hope and comfort from the Great Comforter (John 14:26). Next time you find yourself in the dark valley, know what He says and does for us. He leans in with His steadfast love and faithfulness and whispers, "I'm near to you, Child."

"Lord, I need You!"

66

"COME TAKE YOUR SEAT."

Walking through hardship on this earth is tricky. It always seems to reach a place of influence that robs us of the truth of who we are and where we stand with God. Our eternal identity gets muddled by the weight of a heavy burden, and we get blinded to eternal things by the blunt needs of the flesh we face daily.

Our family had reached a point in our battle with cancer where our entire schedules rotated around doctor appointments, test results, treatment plans, and watching for results. We became so enthralled into caring for the body that we couldn't even see the spirit. One day, as I was trying to sit still before a busy day of appointments and running around, I read Ephesians 2:6, "And raised us up with him and seated us with him in heavenly places in Christ Jesus." I let myself float past this world right up to a seat in the Eternal City, our true forever home, and I thought, "Oh, if we could all just be there, in Heaven right now, together." And then I realized we are. This text doesn't say, "One day…". It's not written in the future tense. We are there. Now. Don't get me wrong. This truth didn't give me a license to erase our schedule that day and skip all our doctor appointments. We still had to go there. We still had to walk this earth, get the treatments, assess them, and readjust the drugs, treatments, etc. And in the end, Mark went Home.

Operating in this truth that today, we are seated with Him in heavenly places sets our eyes on the hope we have in Christ. This insight changes everything. Yes, we are assigned to this earth for a season. And we already know that in this life, we will have trouble (John 16:33). Christ Himself made that clear to us. But to know that we are there with Him because the work He accomplished on the cross has forever sealed our position there changes how we walk here on this earth. Even through struggles. And let's not forget that this means we have access to every spiritual blessing in the heavenly places through Christ Jesus (Ephesians 1:3-4).

Knowing that we are seated in heavenly places with Christ and that we have every spiritual blessing through Him, we can face what is before us with hope, grace, and even peace. I saw this in Mark. With each new treatment, he trusted God. When we got bad news, he grabbed my hand, and we prayed for His will to be done. None of the pain went away from his body, but the peace that passes understanding set up residency in our hearts and minds. As we meditated on God's word and His truths, we found comfort where no medicine could reach. As you walk through this life today on this earth, remember that you are also seated with Christ in the heavenly places, and through His word and Holy Spirit, you have access to all the spiritual blessings. Reach out, receive, and rest in your true position.

"Lord, remind me of my true position today."

67

"IT IS FINISHED."

This is a quote from Christ we mostly hear around Easter as we reflect on our Savior's death and resurrection. It seems fitting to reflect on these words during Holy Week, but why now? Why is this phrase important in our hardship? Looking at what it means and how it was said sheds light on its significance for us today. This is one of seven phrases recorded that Jesus spoke from the Cross. We're familiar with the others, "Father, forgive them, for they know not what they do" (Luke 23:34), "Truly, I say unto you, today you will be with me in paradise" (Luke 23:43), "Woman, behold your son! Son, behold your mother!" (John 19:26-27), "I thirst" (John 19:28), and "Father, into your hands I commit my spirit" (Luke 23:46). Although each phrase uttered by Christ has meaning and serves a purpose, "It is finished" seems the weightiest.

First, let's look at the other things Christ said on the Cross. We see Him interceding on behalf of His enemies and ask God to forgive them. We also see Christ taking care of His mother. Putting her in the hands of a trusted disciple. We see Christ extending forgiveness to the fullest extent to a sinner who asked Him to remember him. And finally, "I thirst" was said to fulfill the scriptures. These sayings all have a clear purpose in His dialog. But why'd He say, "It is finished"? This statement was really a declaration. Christ was announcing that He accomplished all He had set out to do. Also, let's look at the tense it is written in. Perfect tense. This is used to indicate that not only did it happen, but it was happening during the time Christ said it and is also continuing to happen even now. Christ, who is the same yesterday, today, and tomorrow, accomplished the ultimate work covering the past, present, and future. Nothing else needed to be done for our salvation. No more rules carved in stone or sacrifices of animals or any other life were required. The work was completed. It was finished. Do you know what this means? The greatest need of mankind has already been fulfilled, once and for all. He has made our salvation available to each of us. It is finished. Does this mean we have no more needs? It doesn't. And scripture addresses our needs. "Ask, and it will be given. Seek, and you will find. Knock and the door will be opened" (Matthew 7:7-8). "...for your Father knows what you need even before you ask" (Matthew 6:8). He addresses our needs throughout His Word. But what this does mean is that mankind's greatest need is already met.

As you face your current hardship, which seems insurmountable, let this truth set you free. Our eternal salvation is sealed by the blood of Christ, our Savior. Our current situation, our past, and even what we will face in the future bear no weight on this greatest need we have. All the work is done. Salvation is ours. In the face of your hardship, let your mind rest easy, knowing that your greatest need, a need you could never satisfy by your own will or work, has already been accomplished. Christ, our Savior, has made a place for us with Him for eternity in paradise. He declares we are seated "with Him in Heavenly places" (Ephesians 2:6). Right now. In real time. This acknowledges that our salvation is completed, and whatever hardship, loss, or sorrow we face on this earth at this moment, bears no effect on the finished work of our Savior. We are here, wrestling with this world, and we are there, with Him. Nothing we face now can alter or change our heavenly seat with Abba Father. Let this truth bring comfort in Christ's declaration from the Cross. And know whatever we face, nothing can undo His victory.

"Lord, into Your hands, I commit my spirit."

68

"DO NOT BE AFRAID."

I sat in the waiting room as the eight-hour reconstruction surgery took place. They had removed the tumor and six inches of his tibia with it. The rebuilding began, but I felt like I was being torn down. They say there are three tiers to being afraid; alarmed, frightened, and terrified. I felt them all at that moment, sitting in the waiting room that day. Thoughts of his safety during surgery flooded my mind. Future thoughts of whether they would get all the cancer or if this leg would be strong enough to carry him bombarded my mind. And I felt as if I were sinking into a deep, dark pit. I was afraid. Yet, as I sat, scripture came floating to the surface of my mind.

I didn't even notice it at first, distracted by the ticking clock across the room or the eerie quietness that filled the air. But slowly, eventually, my heart calmed. My mind was focused on His promise. "Fear not, for I am with you; be not dismayed, for I am your God, I will strengthen you, I will help you, I will uphold you with my righteous right hand" (Isaiah 41:10). And just as He did for the Israelites thousands of years ago, He sat beside me, assuring me of His promise in that fearful moment, on that dark day. The reality is that God's greatness and faithfulness are not dependent on our ability, strength, or faith. God is God. And He is good. These foundational truths settled me in that waiting room chair, full of fear, questions, and pain. I soaked up His Presence and the truth of the God I serve.

There is a place where hardship takes us where everything we see or can surround ourselves with fades away, and we are left with pure truth. We are not strong enough. And God Almighty is. It's hard to see when we have all our comforts of health, friends, and family around us. When we are winning and gaining ground, and prospering. But in the moments when we have no answers, this is where our great God's words bring the ground back under our feet and stabilize us: "Do not be afraid." In the face of such uncertainty, how can we redirect our fearful hearts and calm our souls? Because of the God we serve. He tells us why we don't have to be afraid. Clinging to Him and believing His word becomes a safety net of faith when our circumstances make the truth hard to grasp. When our hearts feel faint, standing on His Word can recenter us. I find saying His promises out loud or listening on a Bible app can bring my bleeding heart back into focus on whom I belong to. This brings my heart the courage to believe again.

First of all, it's Who we trust in. The God of the universe. The One True God. The Giver of all life. He is worthy of all our praise, worship, and trust. We can depend on His promises. We can rely on His unfaltering character. When we are weak and fickle, unable to stand, He is strong and reliable and carries out His good plan for us. As we receive His assistance, and rest in who He is, an unexplainable assurance comes over us as we realize He is our ever-present help in times of need (Psalm 46:1). It's all about Him.

The God who never changes tells us to give Him our fear and receive from Him His Word. When you are afraid, place your fears in His faithful hands, let His truth comfort you, calm your weary mind, and fill your circumstance with the hope of who He is. And do not be afraid.

"O Lord, I give You my fear."

69

"I'M YOUR FRIEND."

I can't count the people I have met with skewed views of God. They see him as angry, judgemental, or distant. This partly depends on the type of earthly dad you have/had growing up. Or possibly plain old misinformation from a wayward pulpit. And I can't count the damage this causes between our Creator, Abba Father, and us. I have known isolation in our battle with cancer. We stopped getting invited after having to say no enough times. People don't want to be around such pain. I mean, what do you say to someone hurting? And it can feel like we're suddenly on our own. "But there is a friend who sticks closer than a brother" (Proverbs 18:24b).

In all the hardship and emotional draining an illness can bring, we came to know and rely on the truth in this proverb. To know His love in the darkest sadness and trying times is to truly grasp His friendship with us. He does not judge us in our grief. He is not angry with us. Nor is He distant. In fact, He is near to the brokenhearted (Psalm 34:18).

He pulls us close as an intimate friend. His track record with us personally and with all of mankind bears witness to the peace we experience in His presence. As we ponder His nearness and all of His promises, our minds find perfect peace. It is this peace, His peace, that anchors us. The truth is, sometimes life gets too heavy, even for those around us. They don't know what to say or how to help, causing them to become distant and less available. It hurts, no doubt, but humans have their limitations.

If we're honest, we know that from our own shortcomings. When we suffer, there is a place where only our God can comfort us. In this moment, He reaches out His hand and extends His friendship to us. He loves us so. He is the lover of our soul. He alone can sustain us and carry us. He is our faithful Friend. When hardship leads us to a lonely place, and those around us fail us, let's look to Him and be comforted.

Let the friendship of the God of the Universe surround us, and hold us close. Sit in His presence, and allow Him to befriend you. Meditate on His closeness to you and let Him minister to you through His Holy Spirit. Let your mind intentionally imagine Him loving you as His friend. And let go of all the wrong views we have of the One who gave His life for us on a cruel cross so that we might be in communion with Him again. He calls us Friends. Let that truth console you as you trust your heart to Him in your hardship.

"Lord, You are my Friend."

70

"I'M PREPARED FOR THIS."

I'm sure you've heard it said that nothing surprises God. This saying never meant more to me than in my grief. Knowing He was not surprised by my loneliness or Mark's death gave me the security I needed. In times of hardship, the truth that God is prepared for whatever comes our way can bring such assurance. When the enemy tries to get us to focus only on ourselves and our own feelings, an internal struggle to remember that God has a plan arises within us. His plan remains even in the uncertainty that accompanies loss. Remembering that God already knows what happens in our future and is preparing us for whatever comes our way can be a lifeline for our weary hearts. We can get a narrow vision, which leads to isolation and eventually hopelessness. We feel forgotten. But God tells us He has known each of our days before they happened. That is when resetting our minds is crucial. He tells us in this life, we will have trouble (John 16:33). He knows what we are facing. And still, He takes us through it. If He has recorded every one of our days in His book before time began, then we are seen, and what we face serves a purpose.

There is a time to just be in our grief. To face it head-on. And let the emotions flood our hearts. The problem is we can't stay there, or we self-implode. And our Savior knows this. He puts purpose into our struggle. He comes alongside us as we grieve. He sends us ministering angels to comfort us in our time of need (Psalm 91:11-12). He tells us that in our struggle, He comforts us with a purpose so that we can come alongside someone after us and encourage them from our pain and hardship (2 Corinthians 1:3-4).

The God of the seasons gently reminds us in tough times to "not grow weary in doing good, for in due season we will reap if we do not give up" (Galatians 6:9). This has meaning in our hardship for two reasons.

One, this hard time will change. It won't always be this hard. And two, we will reap a harvest. God will replace loss with harvest. He has prepared for us to struggle by giving us His promises to be with us when things get tough. And to remind us that there is a purpose in our struggle.

Finally, He is ultimately preparing our futures to be with Him in Heaven. One day our troubles will end, and we will be healed, whole, and without pain. In the meantime, we can glorify His Name by helping others. As we surrender our pain to Him, trust His Word, and let Him minister to us, we become ministers ourselves. We are not alone. Our struggles do not surprise Him. And He will use your battle for His glory and to build up others. Take heart, HE has overcome this world (John 16:33). When you feel derailed and ill-prepared for what you are walking through, cling to His Word and know He has prepared for this.

"Lord, Thank You for knowing."

71

"ASK ME."

Asking for help when we are in need seems like such a difficult task. A few lies roll around in our heads, and we may not even recognize them as such. Yet, the enemy uses them to keep us silent, isolated, and at greater risk of defeat. One of those lies is that we are a burden when we need help. That's not how God sees it. He knows what we need even before we ask (Matthew 6:8). He who created us knows that we were born in need. He sent His Son to provide our greatest need, salvation. And still, in our everyday lives, we lack. We were made to be in a community and rely on others in this life. And yet, asking for help seems almost like a defeat.

I remember clearly the ten months of my husband's first chemo regimen. It hit him hard. I could barely keep up with all of his demands as he fought off violent vomiting fits, intense fatigue, and mouth sores. I reached a point where I was unable to focus on feeding the family. I had no time to think of a meal, much less buy groceries, get them home, turn on the oven, and cook. A dear friend staying with us for the week noticed my need. She reached out to our church and set up a MealTrain through them. The response was overwhelming. For the next ten months, our church family and community brought food to our door, prepared, hot, and ready to serve. Mark and I felt like we were being a burden. Thoughts of "Why can't we do this simple task for our family?" flooded our minds, even as we struggled to keep food in Mark's belly. But as the days went by, and we saw the faces of so many light up as they helped us meet this basic need, we realized we were not a burden but an avenue in which some could serve. Those who brought us meals were genuinely grateful to have been able to bless us in our struggle. And what a blessing it was!

Mark and I wanted to be able to handle that season on our own.

I guess pride had something to do with that. And yet, some strong friendships were grown out of this opportunity to be served by others. In our time of need, God puts us in the hearts of others, allowing them to love through service. It strengthened their faith in a good God and helped those in need tremendously. So, ask God when you are in need. And let Him work both in you and in others.

Another lie that keeps us from asking is that God does not care about our needs. It can feel this way as we struggle with a heavy load, but it's simply not true. When we ask God in our time of need, we see how lavishly He provides for us. Ten months of meals for a family of six is no small task. Yet, when God stepped in, we were overflowing with delicious meals, gift cards for the kids to use for after-practice snacks, and new friendships that blossomed in the meantime. We needed food. He provided so much more. And a community rallied around one family. It was more than we asked for. That's the generous God we serve.

When you are in need, ask your Heavenly Father. And watch what He provides. He loves us. He sees us. His heart is for us. Ask.

"Abba, I have a need."

72

"YOU ARE MINE."

Hardship rattles our entire life. We are drained of physical strength and mental clarity, and even our identity is questioned at times. There is so much going on that we can forget who we are. Several years into our battle with cancer, I felt myself losing who I was. I was depleted of sleep, energy, and even hope. I noticed I was more curt, ill-tempered, and not my usual, pleasant self. I also had no time to exercise so I didn't even look like myself. I enjoy eating healthy foods, but had no time to cook. I found myself eating stuff I would never eat. It seemed this hardship was turning me into someone else altogether. I felt lost in someone else's life. I was listening to and relying on my own interpretation of what was going on. And that internal voice can be so deceiving. Who was I before the hardship? Am I still her? It seemed unclear.

I was blessed to have Mark as my husband. He was so intentional in encouraging me, to love me unconditionally, and yes, to correct me when he saw me slipping into something that did not represent me or my Savior. He cared about me on an intimate level, always supporting me, and always involved in my life. One who says the hard stuff and is always willing to step up and be there for his bride. Even in my times of ugliness when I let my emotions get the best of me and I got short-tempered or even rude, Mark loved me well. That's a good husband. Flawed, human, but a great helper. He represented the role of "husband" very well in our twenty-five years of marriage. Yet, after Mark left, my attention was drawn to the idea of Christ, the Husband of the Church. I hadn't thought about Jesus in that role much before then. But now that Mark is gone, this title for Christ caught my attention.

So, what is God saying to us in our difficult times? He says, "Let me tell you who you are." Isaiah 62:11 is a beautiful proclamation of who we are in Him. "Behold, the Lord has proclaimed to the end of the earth; Say to the daughter of Zion, Behold your salvation comes; behold, His reward is with him, and his recompense is with him. And they shall be called The Holy People, The Redeemed of the Lord, and you shall be called Sought Out…" The Lord Himself calls us daughters of Zion, Holy, Redeemed by Him. We are His, even in trials. Even when we don't feel like we are. He is saying this to the Jewish people, and He says it to us today. We are His. This is our grounding in times of uncertainty. When we forget who we are, we can remember that He claims us as His own, as is, because He says so. No circumstance can change that.

The enemy tries to take our true identity in Christ away when we are weak. He tries to replace truth with his lies that we are somehow no longer sons or daughters when we struggle. But he doesn't have the authority to do so. Why does he try to convince us of this? So we will turn away from the One who loves us and has claimed us as His own. Then we feel alone and without hope. Remember, the enemy means to kill, steal, and destroy (John 10:10). But thanks be to God, He has proclaimed that we are His. And what God has brought together, no one can tear apart (Matthew 19:6).

Christ, the Groom of the church, is our husband. Holding fast to this truth in our struggle strengthens us. It reminds us that as God's sons and daughters, we are heirs to all He has for us (Galatians 4:6). That is our hope in the darkest of times. He is our help because He has decided that we are His. Whenever you are down, under the weight of sorrow and grief, look up, your Father says, "You are Mine."

"Christ, I am Yours."

73

"I'M GETTING THINGS READY FOR YOU."

I just spent time with my adult kids for the holiday. Since my husband passed away, our family has grown. Three of my kids are now married, and one has my first grandchild. We went out on a pontoon together, laughed, soaked in the sun, and enjoyed the day. It was bittersweet because Mark loved setting up pontoon days each year. He'd reserve the boat, set the menu of snack foods, and get all the things needed to take on the boat to make the day a day to remember for all. He thought of everything. Not only that, but as we went island hopping through the lake that day, he plotted out our every move on a map, steering clear of all sand bars, and even found the path of least resistance. He truly had every detail handled so his family could climb onto the boat, sit back, eat, breathe in the fresh air, and have a great time. The time Mark would spend getting things ready for a boat day made it a perfect experience.

This year it went great. My oldest son took on the job of reviewing the maps for any buoys or sandbars we needed to avoid. He drove us through the day with ease because he was prepared. I know it was a lot on his shoulders, having to be extra alert while the rest of us sat back and enjoyed ourselves. But it was not the same as when Mark got everything ready for us, as he did so many times before. We missed his preparedness. We missed his huge grin from ear to ear as he looked around the boat and soaked in all the smiles and contentment from his family's gratefulness. And that got me thinking about what it means for those on the boat to have someone who has thought out the entire trip. All so we could sit back and know we were cared for.

Abba Father is doing that for us now as He prepares our eternity for us. The price is already paid. As we walk through this world, carrying out His will, He is getting things ready for us. "If I go, and prepare a place for you, I will come again and will take you to myself, that where I am, you also may be" (John 14:3). He has ascended into Heaven and has been getting ready for us to join Him ever since. Matthew 25:34 again states clearly that He is preparing for His own: "Then the King will say to those on his right, 'Come, you who are blessed by my Father, inherit the kingdom prepared for you from the foundation of the world." And again, in Hebrews 11:16b, there is a city that has been prepared for us in advance: "...Therefore, God is not ashamed to be called their God, for he has prepared for them a city."

Our eternity is not going just to happen one day. Since the foundation of the earth, He has seen this day. He has been preparing a Holy city for us! And He waits for us with anticipation! On your hardest day, look up. He is preparing for us!

"Lord, I await Your return!"

74

"HERE I COME, CHILD!"

It seems there's always so much debate on when the Lord will return. But there is one thing I know, definitively. He is returning. Our Lord and Savior has not forgotten us. He is readying His horse even now and will come back here to take us to be with Him forever. Amen! I say, Maranatha (which means, "Our Lord, come!) bibleinfo.com.

I know we can lose sight of this truth in our darkest hours when the weight of grief and loss is so heavy on our chest. All we see is the heaviness right in front of us. It pierces our thinking and immobilizes us. I've been told once you lose someone, it never gets better. This is an exact quote. From whom? From at least one hundred people who have taken the time to share their thoughts on the loss of a loved one. I know you've heard it, too. The profound effect of losing the one you love so dearly is real. It is all-encompassing. It stays with you. I agree to that degree. I will never be the same person I was before I had to say goodbye to my husband. Yet, it does get better.

I know this to be true based on the promise that Christ is returning. One day, we will be reunited with our loved ones who belong to the Lord. One day our wounds of loss and grief will be healed, and we will be made whole. It will get better. And I believe that as we lay our broken hearts at the foot of the Cross and entrust Christ with our aching souls, He heals us, speaks truth into our loss, and mends what is broken here on this earth. This is not based on my wishful thinking that the pain will subside or a Pollyanna mentality from a place of ignorance. Psalm 147:3 addresses brokenness: "He heals the brokenhearted and binds up their wounds." Psalm 34:18 says, "He is close to the brokenhearted."

There were countless nights when God did just this for my broken heart. As I surrendered to the inability to heal Mark, rescue our kids from the traps the enemy set for them, or even make my body sleep so I could face the next day, I would lay in His presence without anything to offer up, just my broken heart. In His presence, He calmed my fears, settled matters I had no power to control, and soothed my open wounds. It didn't make any of the heartaches go away. But through His healing presence, I was able to rest and let Him refresh my weary mind and body. Psalm 34 goes on to say, "When the righteous cry for help, the Lord hears and delivers them from all their trouble" (Psalm 34:19). God doesn't heal partially. He doesn't address one need. Abba Father heals us entirely. Every ache in every area of our life. He is the Provider, Protector, and Comfort of our soul. He sees our struggle and comes to our rescue. Scripture also tells us it will get better. "Those who sow in tears shall reap with shouts of joy! He who goes out weeping, bearing seed for sowing, shall come home with shouts of joy, bringing his sheaves with him" (Psalm 126:5-6).

In your moment of pain and suffering, remember this truth: He welcomes our sorrow. He takes it and calms our spirits. When we go to Abba with our brokenness, He heals. When we are hurting, as we lift our souls to Abba Father, we can trust His word and know His promises to be true. In this life, on this earth, we can know the healing and comfort of a loving God. And then there is the hope we cling to. He is returning. He is preparing a place for us by His side in Heaven. We know there are no tears, no disease, no suffering in Heaven (Revelation 21:4). That is where He is taking us when He comes for us. So, hold on in your distress. Look up, and meditate on His truth. He loves you. He sees you. He is coming for you.

"Abba, Maranatha!"

75

"I WILL MAKE IT RIGHT."

After Mark went Home, I started noticing something. Lives were being lost to cancer. Whenever there was a call for prayer requests, it was as if every one of those requests centered around someone having cancer. Nieces. Nephews. Children. Neighbors. It honestly became a trigger for me. I would have to excuse myself from the meeting. This brought doom and indignation to me. I felt trapped in a world lost to this disease. Hardship can do this to us. It can shift our thinking and change our view of this world. Cancer is just one of those injustices we deal with in our world. Sin has opened the gates for all kinds of wrongs that plague our world. And it can feel defeating, especially if we are touched by injustice ourselves. The enemy would have us sit in that loss. He can take a piece of truth and make it our focus, distracting us from God's promises.

The truth is, there is injustice everywhere. So, how can we guard our hearts against slipping into a hopeless feeling of our personal world and the world at large? We can renew our minds with His Word. Revelation 21:4 says, "He will wipe every tear from their eyes and death shall be no more, neither shall there be mourning, nor crying, nor pain anymore, for the former things have passed away." He is working to this end for us, for His glory, despite all the hurt and pain we see and even experience on this earth. This is His promise to us. Whether it is a disease or a person, God will avenge us on our behalf. With these human eyes, we must remember that there is more than just what we see happening around us. Even though we can't see His Spirit, He is working around us, through us, and in our lives. Because He is holy and just, He can't let injustice remain. We can trust that our Holy God will make all wrongs right. For His glory. Let that be our peace of mind.

As we fix our minds on His word, our thinking about our sin-sick world changes. His truth can let us see our circumstances through a new lens; His victory, His power, His will being carried out through His sovereignty. We can begin this shift in our thinking through His Word. This can be accomplished through daily practice, of course. But when we can't give that time or focus daily, He still uses His Word to transform us. Whenever we open His Word, its power penetrates our thinking and enlightens us with His truth. Trust the power of His Word more than you do your own ability to devote scheduled time to it. Remember, He meets us where we are. In your distress, dive into His word and be reminded that God will make things right for us.

"Lord, I trust in You."

IV.
HOW HE FEELS
(ABOUT US)

With hardship comes emotions. We are sad, overwhelmed, and even hopeless at times. We can be confused, tired, and frustrated. These are common emotions to all humans. Made in His image, we know God our Father has emotions as well. Taking time to meditate on how our Creator God feels about us is life-giving, especially in our hardship. Knowing what He feels about us will allow us to properly process our own feelings and silence the tactics of the enemy to destroy us with our own emotions, creating space to feel without a need to escape, isolate, or believe lies in our vulnerable human emotions.

76

HE WANTS US

Have you ever let yourself think about how your Creator God wants you for Himself? How does He long to be in the right relationship with you? If you have accepted Him as your Savior, you know His desire is for mankind to return to Him and be His children. But that desire for us is not just a one-time longing. His heart is toward us. Lamentations 3:22 tells us, "The steadfast love of the Lord never ceases; his mercies never come to an end." He finds delight in us (Psalm 18:19). In the Garden, after Adam and Eve ate the fruit and were hiding from God because of their sin, God's response was a longing and an aching that their closeness had been compromised. "Where are you?" (Genesis 3:9). This question was not spoken in anger or disbelief. God knew that man would sin. But his heart ached at the separation sin puts between Him and us. He knew their sin would stop the intimate walk in the Garden until one day when we would be reunited with Him in Paradise. He knew His Son would have to pay the price so we could be reunited with Him. He loves being near His children, like a good Father. He knows the divide our disbelief and sin can cause. And His heart hurt at the separation.

Sometimes hardship can blind us to our Loving Father as well. It can cause us to withdraw from our Heavenly Father as our hearts break with pain. In our time of need, it's so inspiring to think about His love for us and His longing to have us as His own. Our hardship can separate us or it can draw us closer to Him. What we focus on. What we think about. These can encourage our nearness to Abba Father or it can cause a divide between us and Him.

I was sitting in my sunroom one night, maybe on the edge of withdrawing from my Heavenly Father, when my husband walked into the room. He was tired and hurting, but he walked in with a smile. In desperation, I asked, "Why the smile?" and he looked at me and said, "Isn't it amazing to think that our God wants to be with us? After a long day of doubts, questions, and concerns, he wants to sit in this sunroom with us. He isn't hiding from us. Isn't resenting our questions. He's still calling us His own." And he wrapped his arms around me and said, "Tina, we are so blessed to have a good Father helping us through this." Mark had spent the day thinking about God's goodness. I had spent the day reeling in the hardship. God was with us both. I was exhausted. But Mark was smiling.

Knowing that God wants us regardless of our circumstances will lighten the load. It will give us hope and encouragement. It will give us the right perspective on what truth is. He wants us. Always. No matter what.

Let your Father's true heart pour out His unconditional acceptance and love in your sunroom today.

"Lord, pull me in with Your love."

77

HE IS PLEASED WITH US

When we are struggling with difficult times in our lives, we tend to measure our worth by how we are doing. How we are handling the situation. How our attitude is as we struggle. How well we can keep everything together. Are our house, our finances, and our faith in order? We can begin to think we don't measure up. And that can lead us to feel like God is displeased. When the stress of everyday life becomes too much, we forget where our worth is anchored.

I have one vivid memory of feeling like I was not measuring up under the stress of a particular time in our battle with cancer. It was the end of the school year and I had two graduating from school. One from 8th grade and one from high school. We had wrestled through the final college applications and all the parties of celebration for both children. A senior trip was planned for the whole family. Then my senior came home with a severely sprained ankle. How'd that happen? I barely cooked that week, and the laundry had aged so much it was now talking to me whenever I walked by.

One afternoon, as I was walking in circles trying to figure out where to spend the 15 minutes I had before racing to pick up my 8th grader from a half day of school, I let my shoulders sink and said out loud, "I'm sorry, Lord." Sorry, my house was a mess. Sorry, I hadn't fed my family a cooked meal. Sorry, I was dreading a vacation we had not even gone on yet. And sorry I was so disappointed in a God who stayed by my side. My prayer turned into tears. I sat down on the kitchen floor, tears flooding my eyes. Clearly, I was not doing anything well. Then, I thought of the verse where a voice from heaven came booming through the clouds as the Father looked at Jesus, "This is my Son in whom I am well pleased" (Matthew 3:17). And it hit me. My heart skipped a beat as I reached for my Bible. How had I missed this all these years? To confirm what I thought was true, I read it again. God announced His good pleasure in His Son before He endured the cruel cross. Before He stormed the gates of Hell and took the keys back from the enemy. Before any of this, God was pleased with Jesus, His Son. And I heard God whisper to me, "You are still my daughter."

His love for me does not depend on how well I feed my family or stay on top of all the laundry. His love is not even dependent on my attitude. He loves me because I am His own. And nothing changes my daughtership. Not when I am slaying laundry or cooking gourmet meals every night. Not when I muster enough courage to get through a day without tears filling my eyes. Not when I have the best attitude. His love is unconditional. He is pleased with us because we are His.

When we find ourselves in a slump, it's hard to see our worth and this truth can seem murky. Think of a small child making a total mess as they attempt to create a gift for mom or dad. They've spilled the paint all over the table, spread glue all over their seat, and have paper cuttings stuck to the scissors, carpet, and sliding glass doors. They're a hot mess, but as they lift up their treasure to honor Mom, your heart melts. Mess? What mess? "Look at what my child made for me." It's not hard to see this mother's pleasure found in her child. And when we take a breath and lift up our own mess, God responds the same way. He loves us. "Mess? What mess? Look at my daughter. My treasure." When you feel your life has become a big mess, listen for His voice whispering His love for you, His daughter.

"Abba, Thank You for Your love."

78

HE CHOOSES US

To be chosen changes everything. Let's say you're given a task and it's a lot of work. Maybe complicated, too. It's going to take time, energy, and effort. But then your boss peeks his head into your office and says, "Hey, just so ya know, I chose you for this job because I know you, and you're perfect for it..." And you perk up. Or remember when you were chosen by your spouse. Out of all the other fish in the sea, they chose you. How about when you're holding your child, and it hits you that out of all the parents in the world, God chose you to bring this one up in His ways? This knowledge changes everything.

When we feel ill-equipped, insufficient, or incapable but have been chosen, it boosts our confidence. The decision was calculated for reasons that may not be clear to us. Let's look at the chosen people of God. Deuteronomy 14:2 says, "For you are a people holy to the Lord your God, and the Lord has chosen you to be a people for his treasured possession, out of all the people who are on the face of the earth." There is nowhere to point that explains why God chose this people group. They were simple, common folks, but He wanted a nation to show who He was. So, He chose the Israelites.

Now, let's look at the twelve disciples. Is there one you could point to explaining why Christ chose them? No. Sure, they were common fishermen, tradesmen, a doctor, but then tax collectors...? Common folk. They didn't stand out for anything good, at least. Yet Christ chose them, and they believed. And He began His Church through them. In 1 Peter 2:9 (NKJV), we see the purpose of this chosen generation, "But you are a chosen generation, a royal priesthood, a holy nation, His own special people, that you may proclaim the praises of Him who called you out of darkness into His marvelous light." When something is chosen, it is to serve a purpose. For those whom God has chosen, this is true as well. We are to proclaim His praises. But what about when we get derailed by life? What happens when we face hardship head-on? We are still called by God for His glory.

So, even in your tired, weary state, there is purpose. You're still called for His glory. How do we walk in this truth? By resting in Him. Knowing He has chosen us even in this time. Allow yourself space to recognize that you are chosen by the Almighty and you are human and imperfect. God does not want perfection. He wants you. We are not always chosen to have it all together. Rather, to bring Him glory. We can do that when we struggle. Trusting in His promises, relying on His strength in our weakness. Believing His word. When we struggle, let's keep our hearts focused on the joy of our salvation. Let's remember, we are chosen.

"Lord, I am Yours. Use me."

79

HE CONNECTS WITH US

Connection. A strong bond. It's what every human craves. It's what we need to be healthy. Yet, often, the opposite can be formed in grief or hardship. A disconnect. A division between us and the ones we go to for support. For my family, our battle with cancer lasted eight years. People who knew us and even connected with us were there for us for many of those years. But our change of schedule, whenever we needed more care, caused a separation. Mark was unable to be at work. Doctor appointments were an hour or hours away. We even took trips out of the country when additional care was needed. Our simple schedule change caused us to be disconnected from those we would normally connect with. They could not be with us during those times, and we felt it.

And then there were the unrelatable ripple effects of dealing with cancer. Food became more of a task instead of a social event to center around. The kids grew weary of dealing with all of the changes and just wanted a break. They found themselves out visiting friends more. Mark and I felt disconnected at times in our hardship. This can happen. We feel separated from our sphere of support. But God presses into our hardship. He can go with us. His word tells us He is with us always, to the end of the age (Matthew 28:20b). The Omniscient Good Father is with us always. In the doctor's office. On the plane, as we head out of town. When we are home alone.

I love the name Emmanuel given to our Savior, Jesus. God is with us. He stays connected when we can't. He knows what we need, as He created us. He knows our circumstances and needs before we even ask Him (Matthew 6:8). He sees our need for genuine connectedness and meets us wherever our grief takes us because He loves us. Because He promised us He would. Because He cares for us. This is a concept God taught me well before cancer, or even being married to Mark. As a child, my family moved often. As my siblings got older and moved on, I was always the new girl, without friends. God showed me that in every move, and every new school, He was my constant. He remained with me, Emmanuel with each new place.

Fast forward to the hardship of enduring a cancer battle with Mark, and God showed me again that He remains. He stays with us. Not up in the sky, looking down at us, but walking in the hardship alongside us. It's important to remember that our difficulties do not take us away from God. Romans declares that nothing shall separate us from His love. Nothing. This list is all-encompassing: "For I am sure that neither death nor life, nor angels nor rulers, nor things present nor things to come, nor powers, nor height nor depth, nor anything else in all creation, will be able to separate us from the love of God in Christ Jesus our Lord" (Romans 8:38-39).

Knowing this truth can bring our emotions in check and calm our hearts, regardless of our circumstances. Take heart when our hardship prevents us from connecting with the ones we love and rely on. The One who created you pulls you in. He connects to us. He remains when those around us cannot.

"Emmanuel, let nothing separate us."

80

WE ARE THE
APPLE OF HIS EYE

The origin of the saying, "the apple of His eye," began with the King James translation of the Bible. It dates back to 1611 and is a fascinating expression of the Father's love for His own. When He declares we are "the apple of His eye," He's saying so much more than the fact that He adores us, though that truth alone baffles me and humbles me. Why does God even care to know me, much less want a relationship with me? When we struggle, we can feel less of His love. A tactic of the enemy but a lie nonetheless. So what does it mean to be the apple of His eye?

In Hebrew, it translates as "little man of the eye." This refers to the tiny reflection of oneself that is seen in someone else's eye. Ever seen that? You're gazing into the eyes of your loved one, and you notice that you see your own reflection in their eye. Think of the physical closeness that is required to see your reflection in someone's eye. Can you count on one hand how many people you would let get that close to you physically? I don't even need one whole hand. That space is reserved for the intensely intimate few. A spouse, and maybe kids. Can you hear the invitation for intimacy here?

To see your reflection in His eye, He pulls you in, really in. Super close to Him. And that's where He wants you. Because you're that great? No, friend. Because He is that great. We see this phrase in three other places in God's Word. In Psalm 17:8, David reminds God to keep us as the apple of His eye. Can we do that? Can we remind God of His promises? Absolutely. Because when we do that, we are proclaiming His own truth. And that reminds us as well. If we're honest, He doesn't need reminding. We do. "Keep me as the apple of Your eye." David desperately needs God to pull him intimately close. To know his heart. To save, protect, and rescue him from his enemies. What is he banking on? Is David banking on his own goodness? No. God's goodness. His promises to us. This is what He says He will do. Rescue. Protect. Save.

Proverbs 7:2 paints a slightly different image of a loving father instructing his precious son: "Keep my teachings as the apple of your eye." Again, the call to intimately hold the father's instruction so close you can see the "little man," the reflection of his father, in the son's eye. Closeness. Full access to one's soul. Lamentations 2:18 is a plea from God's people to "let not the apple of thine eye cease" (KJV). Once we fully grasp this intimate position God Himself desires of us, we realize we can't live without it.

We need a Savior. He says, "I am He." Why? Because it's who He is. Oh, praise Him. It's not based or rooted whatsoever in what we bring to the relationship. It's all Him. The next time you hear this phrase, take a second and soak in its full message to you. You are the apple of His eye!

"Lord, keep me as the apple of Your eye."

81

HE COUNTS
THE HAIRS ON OUR HEAD

"Why, even the hairs of your head are numbered. Fear not; you are more valuable than many sparrows" (Luke 12:7). What a strange verse, right? Again, in Matthew 10:30 it says, "But the very hairs of your head are numbered." Why is this true? And why does it matter? Good questions. The first is easy. God knows the number of hairs on our heads because He cares. He cares about you. He is so tuned in to you, your needs, your wants, your struggles, joys, and yes, your pain. He loves you. Not like the world loves. The world loves pizza and ice cream and drama and horror. It loves pumping us full of "if it feels good, do it" empty messages that leave us reeling for more. It "loves" you into self-righteousness, self-pity, or self-destruction. That is not love.

God loves us with everlasting love (Jeremiah 31:3). His love for us sent His Son willingly to the Cross to set us free and draw us back into the right relationship with our Creator God, His Son, and His Holy Spirit. God's love is what changes our hardened, sin-sick hearts into clay for His healing, rejuvenating, and shaping for our good. His love has no limits, strings, or end. He demonstrates this love for us "in that, while we were yet sinners, Christ died for us" (Romans 5:8). That's why this is true. So why does it matter to us that God counts the hairs on our heads?

Have you ever held someone so dear to you that you just gazed at them? Studied them? Sat with them, enjoying them? How about a parent or grandparent or a child? My mom was a dynamic woman of God. She was beautiful, approachable, and engaging. A true treasure! I have vivid memories of watching her talk with a neighbor, a hurting friend, or a stranger. She would act like that person was the only person around and love them well. I studied her eyes as they were fixed on whomever she was with. I was amazed at how loving and attentive she was. Her crystal blue eyes and curly strawberry-blond hair drew me in and captured my attention. She was a treasure to me, and I memorized her face. I also hold as dear treasures each one of my four children. When they were tiny, I would hold them close and try my best to memorize their features, amazed at Abba's generosity in giving me these treasures. I have cherished them dearly, from crooked smiles to sleepy eyes. I know my kids by the back of their heads, even.

Our Heavenly Father knows us even better than that. He knows our hearts (Luke 16:15a) and every detail about us. Physically, yes, and emotionally, mentally,and spiritually. He knows us better than we know ourselves. And this shows us His Father's heart. We are His treasures. We are His prized possessions. He adores us. These strange verses about the hairs on our heads are in the Bible to remind us how He loves us and how He feels about us. When we are weighed down by our struggles, remembering that He knows the number of hairs on our heads can bring comfort and assurance that if He knows such a trivial thing about us, He knows our deepest needs.

"Lord, You know me well."

82

HE THINKS HIGHLY AND OFTEN OF US

I've been learning from Abba Father about the self-narrative we get stuck in our heads, especially when we are in hardship. It's a cruel, self-defeating narrative that is not based on truth. Rather, it's the enemy's playground to deceive us and convince us we are unworthy, unfit, or just unable to get through something hard. Every human soul is familiar with this. It goes something like this, "You're going back again for forgiveness on this same sin? You're not strong enough to get through this. This time, you will fail. This will be the end of you." You've heard these lies in your head, I am sure. The tricky lies are the ones with a tiny bit of truth interwoven into them. Are we worthy, on our own? Are we strong enough, on our own? No. That is true. But are we alone? Absolutely not. God is thinking of us always.

Scripture tells us in Psalm 139:18, "How precious are your thoughts about me, O God. They cannot be numbered! I can't even count them; they outnumber the grains of sand! And when I wake up, you are still with me!" (NLT). This verse magnifies the Father's love for us. He isn't just up there...somewhere. Distant. Aloof. He's thinking about us. He cares what we're going through, thinking, and struggling with. This is crucial to understand as it gives us a proper perspective of our God. If He's thinking about us all the time; joyful thoughts! Too many to count! He will be attentive, available, and thrilled when we go to Him. Not put out, distracted, or disdained by our neediness. In fact, He welcomes it. "Cast all your anxiety on God, because he cares for you" (1 Peter 5:7 NIV). I love how this translation calls it what it is; anxiety.

When my family was going through Mark's amputation, it felt

like every need we had brought us anxiety. Our trials can cast a dark shadow on our basic needs. They cast an even darker shadow when we have an unusual amount of them. In times of hardship, our neediness tends to increase. Anxiety. Lack. Whatever we call it, He welcomes it. He welcomes us. In your struggle. In your time of need. Whenever you look to God, know that He's always thinking about you. All day, all night. And His thoughts toward you are good ones. He waits with open arms to meet your needs, hug your neck, and be your Heavenly Father. Let this truth drown out the self-narrative, full of twisted lies, and lean on His truth. Listen to what He says about you. See Him as approachable, available, all-sufficient, Abba Father.

"Abba, thanks for thinking of me."

83

HE VALUES US

In my times of struggle, I have found that I can feel less-than. I can feel like I have fewer resources, or have less to offer than I usually do. It seems when I am hurting, I have less to give. I can handle less. Sleep less. And it's all I can do to just get up and do the bare minimum for the day. The amount of effort it takes just to brush my teeth baffles me. So I do less. Then I feel less. The problem with this economy is that it's faulty. In this state of mind, I see my worth as what I contribute. I'm only as good as what I can do, for myself, my family, and others. I see my value as what I can bring to the table. Is this how God values us? No, my friend. It's not. We know God values us. He gave His Son for us. But what does it mean to say God values us? And does that include when we have nothing to give? Let's go to His word for this one.

Psalm 139:13-15 sheds powerful light on this topic. I'd say it leaves no room for misinterpretation. "For you formed my inward parts; you knitted me together in my mother's womb" (vs. 13). This is not some distant God. He formed us in our mother's womb. He took the time to put us together. He created us. Verse 14 continues, "Wonderful are your works; my soul knows it very well." He puts value on us by His creativity. We aren't all the same. We aren't thrown together. Rather, we were intricately woven in the depths of the earth (vs. 15). This passage makes it crystal clear that God valued us as we were being formed. Let me point out that was before we believed in Him. Before we did anything for Him or anyone else. He values us because we are His, not for our performance. In Genesis 1:27, we see God made us in His image; to look like Him, to reflect Him in us. He wants us to look at each other and see glimpses of Him. We represent Him when we look like Him. Like a son who is a spitting image of his father, that's how He made us to be. He put

His image on us. Before we spoke a word or did a load of laundry. Before we could serve, even. He valued us by making us in His likeness.

We see in John 10:10 another truth about how God values us. "The thief comes only to steal and kill and destroy; I have come that they may have life. And have it to the full." God wants us to live life abundantly. He came so we could not just live, survive, or exist. No! We're more valuable to Him than that. He came so we could live lavishly in Him. For Him. To be like Him to those around us. He values us because we are His. Made in His image, for His glory. Know that He values you when you can't seem to measure up. Just as you are.

"Lord, I am Your valuable child."

84

WE'RE WORTH DYING FOR

John 3:16 tells it all: "For God so loved the world, that He gave His only Son, that whoever believes in him should not perish but have eternal life." God loves us. He put a value on us, enough to have his only son die a cruel death so that we might be saved from eternal damnation and live forever with Him. Does that not stop you in your tracks? It humbles me.

Our family had so many questions as we walked through the horrible battle of cancer with Mark. Why Mark? Why now? Why cancer? God, where are You? Those kinds of questions can cause a person to question their worth. Does God care that we are down here, suffering? Do we matter to Him? Deep, faith-shattering questions. We walked this path with our kids as they asked them. At times, I asked them. And what we found, again and again, is that He does care. He values us so deeply. He put us in the hearts of neighbors, our church family, and sometimes strangers to rally around us and provide help and encouragement. He met us at just the right time, with just the right amount of strength and compassion through a nurse, or using Mark and myself to have the needed patience or words to say to uplift one another. Our friends showed up for our kids and picked them up, and the school gave them grace on a deadline with a school project, or grace with a bad attitude because of a difficult day they were experiencing. These were all the ways He showed us His care for us in our struggles.

Our greatest need, eternity, was met long before we were even brought into this world. God prepared in advance for a redemptive work that would save us for eternity. He decided the plan to send His Son to the cross, to die for me, Mark, our children, and all He created, long before He ever created Adam or Eve. Before He breathed into the first man's lungs, He saw that sin would enter this world and corrupt it and all He created. He saw that mankind would need a Savior. He saw down through the lineage of mankind into our home and knew we would suffer as a result of living in this sin-sick world. And because He loves us, He brought forth His word, proclaiming all of His promises to come alongside us in our time of need.

He was able to equip us and surround us with all we needed so that we could cling to His garment and rest in His promises. He chose to be with us every step of the way, even when we walked away from Him. He loved us and protected us and forgave us when, by His Spirit, we turned to Him for saving again and again. He knew we would question and fight against His good plans. He saw in advance how we would panic, lose heart, and seek other ways to comfort and cope with the hardships of this world. And He deemed us worth dying for still. Still. Even in our lack. Scripture makes crystal clear how He feels about us: "While we were still sinners, Christ died for us" (Romans 5:8).

Our salvation was planned when God put worth on us. Not anything we could ever earn. Not when we are fully believing and trusting in Him. Not when we are questioning and doubting Him. He sees us worthy. That settles the matter with the One who matters most. Know how God sees you when you feel unworthy, and rest in His love.

"Lord, You make me worthy."

85

HE LOVES TO CALM OUR FEARS

After Mark's death, fear took on a whole new entity in my life. I found it strange that after twenty-five-plus years living with Mark, having him beside me each night, I was not afraid to sleep in the big house alone. Mark and I had just become empty-nesters only four months before he died. It was truly just me in the house. Yet, that was not what I wrestled with fear about. Fear crept into my thoughts in the form of my own identity.

If not Mark's wife, who was I? If not the "stay-at-home" mom of four kids, who was I? Fear wrapped itself around my identity. It gripped who I was with a choking strength that kept me up at night and even robbed me of sleep. If I'm honest, fear robbed me of peace in my heart. I also noticed fear demanding my attention in the area of decision-making. Would I make the wrong choice financially, with the kids, in where I should live? It had not been just me for decades. The enemy dripped fear in my ability to make decisions and stand in who I knew I was without Mark there to remind me I was the daughter of the Most High. And I needed my fears to be calmed.

We have a God who loves to calm our fears. Isaiah tells us this in verse 41:10, where God is comforting His people. "Fear not, for I am with you; be not dismayed, for I am your God; I will strengthen you, I will help you, I will uphold you with my righteous right hand." This is the message He gives to His people as they are coming out of hardship. But regardless of where we are in the battle, there can still be fear. At the beginning, in the middle, or even after it's over. It can sneak in through our weaknesses and go unnoticed for a while.

Mark was healed. God had taken him home, given him a new body, and set him in the very presence of God. And now here I am. Trying to walk in my faith without my partner. Mark's battle had ended, but a new one was just beginning for me. I realized I had a decision to make. I could give into the fear, let it define me, and become enslaved to it. Or I could stand on the Word of God, rest in His promises, and let Him take my fear and the lies that came with it, and listen to what He says. I wanted the latter, but how? How do I receive God's calming of all my fears?

The key is to trust. Trust even when we cannot see the results. Even when our feelings of fear remain. David put it this way, "When the cares of my heart are many, your consolations cheer my soul." Psalm 34:4 gives us a key to receiving the consolation God longs to give us: "I sought the Lord, and he answered me and delivered me from all my fears."

When we are afraid, we need only to seek Him. He is waiting, arms open wide, to rush in, comfort us, and remove our fears. Does that mean He removes all the things we will face on this earth? No. But it does mean He covers us with peace beyond our understanding and stands with us through it all. We have Him and His promises with us. He loves to calm our fears and give us His peace. Today, as you wrestle with fears, seek Him. Lay each one at His feet, and let Him do what He loves.

"Lord, here are all my fears."

86

HE SEES US AS FAMILY

Have you ever felt so included, so surrounded by love and encouragement? That's what a good family provides. It could be flesh and blood, or it could be friends who respect and cherish one another. "Behold, what manner of love the Father has lavished on us, that we should be called the children of God! And that is what we are!" 1 John 3:1(NIV). Being a part of a good family makes all the difference in the world. When we are family, we are cared for, treasured, heard, and included. Our identity is wrapped up in our family. I love it when friends are as close as family. It reminds me that they simply chose me.

We have dear friends who have chosen to be our family. Every year, they open their home up to us all. Some are blood, yes. But some they have chosen to include and love unconditionally. They created a place for us in their home. Set a place at the table. And we felt welcomed. Did you know God has done the same thing for us? He chose us. Scripture says He "grafted us in" (Romans 11:17). We are His children, sons, and daughters. Are we blood-related? Through the blood of His Son, yes. Romans 8:17 declares us "heirs of God and fellow heirs with Christ…". And as part of His family, we have an inheritance of eternal life and the assurance that not one thing can separate us from His love (Romans 8:38-39).

These are all promises we gained when we accepted Christ as our Savior. Will we suffer as family members? Absolutely. How will we suffer? If we walk in our faith in God and understand that we are part of His family, we can suffer with greater peace than the world can give. We can rest in the arms of the Almighty and hide under His wings. (Psalm 91:4). Psalm 68:5-6a holds a treasure close to my heart: "A father to the fatherless, a defender of widows, is God in his Holy dwelling. God sets the lonely in families" (NIV). He has saved us from our sin and corrupted flesh and placed us in His Holy family, setting us apart from the world. We are now His. And He cares for us as sons and daughters.

This reminds me of how tenderly and completely my husband cared for us. He was generous and sought ways to help those around him. But when his family was in need, he would've sold the shirt off of his own back to make sure they had what they needed. Knowing what a wonderful father and husband Mark was, and knowing he was only human, puts a perspective on the value, treasure, and gift it is to be accepted into a perfect family, God's family.

God is a good Father who knows exactly what we need, even before we ask. And gives us what we need. He is all-powerful, sovereign, and all-knowing. And He is our Abba Father. It's by "His Spirit of adoption as sons we cry Abba! Father!" (Romans 8:15). When we cry out to our good and perfect Father, He is there for us, meeting our needs, by His compassionate Father's heart. When we feel trapped under the weight of our struggles, cry out to Him.

"Abba! Father!"

87

HE REJOICES OVER US!

"The Lord your God is with you, he is mighty to save. He will take great delight in you, he will quiet you with his love, he will rejoice over you with singing" Zephaniah 3:17(NIV). What a precious image of our God and His delight in us. I love to read this verse when I am in hardship. It resets my mind on what is lovely and good and true. It resets my vision to see my Savior as my lover. It rests my heart on a saving God. It restores my soul. It changes me. This verse is tucked into the back end of a chapter titled "The Future of Jerusalem," and I can't help but see a similarity in my own story.

In times of loss, pain surrounds us. It seems to be everywhere we look. And God sees our pain, too. He bottles up every tear we cry (Psalm 56:8). But God, who sees all at all times and knows all even before it happens, looks at our hardship differently. What He sees causes Him to rejoice over us. We know too much about Him to think He finds joy in our pain. So, when the Israelites were failing and struggling under the rule of Manasseh in Zephaniah, and when we are struggling today, why does God rejoice over us? It's because He sees us. Not just our pain but the finished product, a place where our suffering is taking us. He knows our worth and the joy we bring Him. And that worth and joy is not based on our circumstances. Rather, it is based on who He says we are. The place He is preparing for us. Suffering gets us there.

We hate to suffer. But God sees the purpose of it. He knows what He is doing. As we suffer, growth, surrender, healing, and intimacy bond us with Abba. He tells us we are His. He quiets us with His love. He rejoices over us with singing. He knows that day is coming. He has no doubt. He knows how this ends, with Him, perfect, healed, whole, in paradise, forever worshiping Him. And He rejoices over that day. The future of

Jerusalem. The future of us.

Our future is good. It is the best. It is coming. And, whether we are okay with it or not, the truth is our suffering prepares us for our future. God knows this. He sees us there already. He is outside of time, unlike us. He sees all. We must have faith in it. This verse in Zephaniah is tucked away in the book written to Israel when things looked dismal, dark, and void of good. Can you relate to feeling this way? Does your outlook currently resemble this? When you feel overwhelmed and turn to things not of Him to soothe, comfort, or just escape, He knows the temptation. He loves us in our weakness. And in His perfection, instead of reacting out of human emotions, God reaches in and draws us near to Him. Our humanness reacts imperfectly, but God responds in perfection. He rejoices over us. From someone who has been right there, and felt distant from God, I can tell you, my actions did not waver His celebrating me.

When we fall away in despair, hold on. It gets better. God is rejoicing over us not because we suffer, but because our suffering has purpose. It is bringing us to Him. To a better place. When you see only your pain, let God's love song to you lift your spirits, refresh your hope, and revive your soul.

"Lord, let me hear Your song over me."

88

GOD LOVES US STEADFASTLY

There is love between a husband and wife, a mother or father and a child, or even between friends that is enduring. And it can be a deep, powerful love. But then there is steadfast love. Steadfast; to be resolute, unwavering. This kind of love goes beyond what I think is even humanly possible. We can be resolute to love someone, but we humans waver. With the best of intentions and the grandest of desires, we fail. Human love is limited. It wavers. Only the God of the universe, perfect, Holy, Righteous, is capable of unwavering, steadfast love.

This is what God loves us with. It is love that does not quit. It does not change in resolve or intensity. It is all wisdom to know what is best needed. It is a never-failing love to withstand all obstacles. It's an unconditional love to withstand our sin and unworthiness. Only God can love this profoundly and completely because He is Love. Exodus 15:13 says, "You have led in your steadfast love the people whom you have redeemed."

I love this image of God's steadfast love in dealing with the Israelites. We know their history. We know their unfaithfulness, stubbornness, and arrogance. We see it in our own hearts today. Yet, God led them in His steadfast love. His love never fails. It never changes. He deals with our sins and failures because He is a good Father. But unlike a human father, He never changes His love towards us. Again, in Deuteronomy 7:9, we see clearly this steadfast love. "Know therefore that the Lord your God is God, the faithful God who keeps covenant and steadfast love with those who love him and keep his commandments to a thousand generations." This is how God describes Himself to His people and us.

Let's look at His character described throughout scripture. Lamentations 3:22-23 tells us, "The steadfast love of the Lord never ceases; his mercies never come to an end; they are new every morning; great is your faithfulness." The security found here is in knowing that His love never changes. It doesn't change when we are hurt, angry, confused, or have so many questions. Having His mercy poured out on our circumstances floods us with hope and courage, knowing we are in His care at all times. We see here through these verses in Lamentations God's attributes and what He promises to do for us in our hardship. He is love. Steadfast love. He extends mercy, always. This is who He is. And we reap the benefits of His character in our time of need. Steadfast love and mercy are ours for the taking, because of who God is. And He never changes. We have His Word, and we have His relationship with us. I can look back on all Abba Father has done for me, and I can't help but be thankful.

Our hope is anchored in His faithfulness. Resting in His unwavering, steadfast love brings us peace in our hardship and a knowing that we are loved through it all. Listening to His Word instead of my own self-narrative, which puts conditions on love, has helped my mind stay anchored in Christ. Trusting His word over my feelings at the moment keeps my feet steady and my burden light in turbulent times.

As you allow yourself to focus on His steadfast love, your burden will lighten, your mind will be refreshed, and your heart will be cared for.

"Lord, I am healed in Your steadfast love."

89

HE FEELS GENEROUS TOWARDS US

Sometimes in our grief, we can feel like we are lacking and in need. We feel like we are receiving anything but generosity. But in those times we must look to His word to see God's posture towards us. It is one of great benevolence. "You open your hand; you satisfy the desire of every living thing" (Psalm 145:16). This verse shows us the generosity of our Loving God. It doesn't say that God meets our needs, although we know He does. This verse emphasizes that He satisfies the desires. In times of grief, this lavish generosity is a healing balm for our broken hearts.

I think of how my husband shopped for Christmas gifts. He was a financial advisor and very responsible with our finances. Every year we would discuss a budget we could afford. He would tell me to be sure and stick to that budget. I would. I watched for sales, mulled over what they really needed, not just all they wanted, and felt good about my spending. My birthday is on Christmas Eve, so every year, following a tradition my dad started when I was a kid, Mark would take me out to dinner and then for some last-minute shopping. On that shopping trip, Mark would lavish our kids with gifts. I would tell him I had already spent our allotted amount for gifts, and he would grin as big as he could and say, "I know, but I have more for them!" He had prepared, of course, but the way that man delighted in lavishing them tickles me still to this day. He was so generous. He found such joy in extending beyond what was planned for and diving even deeper into meeting his family's desires.

How much more so does God do this for us? The God of no limits, who knows our deepest desires, and can give what is best for us, dives deep into His unlimited pockets, grins as large as He can, and finds pure joy in satisfying the desires of His children. What a beautiful picture of Abba Father! He is generous towards us. He starts with this generous act in Ephesians 1:7-8, "In him we have redemption through his blood, the forgiveness of our trespasses, according to the riches of his grace, which he lavished on us" His salvation is generous towards us. Then everything else that is good is given freely from His hand. James 1:17, one of my favorite verses, says, "Every good gift and every perfect gift is from above, coming down from the Father of lights, with whom there is no variation or shadow of change."

Do you hear His generosity even in our grief? Even when we struggle with burdens and hardship? No shadow of change. This is who He is, Generous. Isaiah 55 details how generous God is towards His people: "Come, everyone who thirsts, come to the waters; and he who has no money, come, buy and eat!" (verse 1). Hear His joyful, generous heart towards us! He loves to give us all we need and all we desire. He did not spare His own Son but gave Him up for us and feels lavish towards us (Romans 8:32). If you are in need, come and receive from your generous Abba.

"Abba, Thank You!"

90

HE FEELS PROTECTIVE

What does it mean to be protective of someone? To be protective means someone is capable of and intends to shield someone from danger. As David was fleeing for his life from King Saul, he wrote many scriptures acknowledging that God was his protector. He refers to God as his shield, strong tower, refuge, and hiding place. This is throughout the book of Psalms. Psalm 3:3 says, "But you, O Lord, are a shield around me." David believed God's protective hand surrounded him, kept him safe, and sometimes even hid him from his enemy. God was David's protector. In Psalm 5:11, David speaks of God spreading his protection over him. Proverbs 18:10 says, "The name of the Lord is a strong tower. The righteous run to it and are saved."

There is much evidence that God feels protective of us. There are many ways God protects us. He sends his angels to minister to and protect us. My favorite picture of God being protective of us is found in Psalm 91:3-7. Most agree that this psalm was written by Moses, talking about God protecting the Israelites while wandering in the wilderness for forty years. I've been in that area on my trip to Israel. It is not like I had expected.

The terrain is rocky, with sharp, jagged edges everywhere you step. It's not just "hilly." There are highs so high and lows so low you could not take your eyes off the step in front of you, or you'd slip, fall, and cut yourself badly. There's also not a lot of shade. Nothing about this place seems safe. Yet here's what God promises, "For he will deliver you from the snare of the fowler and from the deadly pestilence. He will cover you with his pinions, and under his wings, you will find refuge; his faithfulness is a shield and buckler. You will not fear the terror of the night nor the arrow that flies by day, nor the pestilence that stalks in darkness, not the destruction that wastes at noonday" (Psalm 91:3-6).

God can protect us from the seen and the unseen dangers. He is enough for us. He positions Himself to protect because it's His desire. When we are in hardship, it can leave us feeling vulnerable, but Psalm 91 addresses this well. The image is of Him covering every part of the desert for His people as they wandered. He covers us, too. This does not mean our hardship will go away. Rather, He will protect us in it. Remember the Israelites? Forty years. God didn't remove them from the desert. In fact, the desert, with all its dangers, was crucial in the growth of His people. It was the desert that brought the Israelites back to their need to be protected. That clear truth brought them to God. Not always first, but always ultimately. Even in our need to be protected, we see God's mercy and His provision for us. Our struggles are part of our growth. God protects us as we navigate our desert. He is faithful. He is able. He uses everything, even our need to be protected, to draw us into Him and to bring us to His side. He protects us. Rest in this promise today and know that Abba Father is protecting us even in our struggle.

"Lord, I receive Your protection."

91

HE KNOWS US BY NAME

Have you ever felt insignificant? After Mark died, there were times when I felt invisible. Insignificant to the rest of the world. I felt like the one who knew me best on this earth, my life partner, was gone. And yes, I mattered to my kids, but not to a significant other. Not to one who did life with me daily. From sunup until sundown. He was gone. And I felt unknown. It's a lonely place to feel like you aren't that special person to someone. It took some adjusting and long prayers to realize He knew my name. Even after my soulmate was gone, Abba Father still knows me.

The God of the universe acknowledges His creation, sure. He has made man in His own image. But there is a deeper connection than just creator and created. And after my husband was gone, I began to see evidence that God Almighty knew me, Tina. Personally. Before Mark died, I was aware of this. But after Mark was gone, I came to realize this more powerfully. He doesn't just know me because He created me. He walks with me. From sun up until sundown, He knows my name. He is personally engaged with me. When I sit quietly in His presence, He whispers words of comfort into my anxious mind, meeting each worry with His truth. He is there when I first open my eyes and when I lay my head on the pillow at night. What a comfort this has been for me. Isaiah 43:1 shows us that God knew the Israelite Nation, but more so, he knew them individually: "But now thus says the Lord, he who created you. O Jacob; he who formed you, O Israel; 'Fear not, for I have redeemed you; I have called you by name, you are mine." He knew the nation, and He knew each one as He formed them in the womb. That is the personal God we serve.

It's hard to put the treasure of this truth into words after losing the person on earth you feel most known by. In my loss, God came closer and called me by name. Throughout God's word, He calls us by name, individually. He called Abraham to leave his home and become a father to nations. He called Samuel by name in the middle of the night to become a great prophet. He called Moses by name from a burning bush to deliver His people from slavery. He called Mary to give birth to the Savior of the world. He calls us by name. He knows us personally. Even when we feel forgotten, lonely, or insignificant, we are significant to Him. John 10:3b puts it this way: "...The sheep hear his voice, and he calls his own sheep by name and leads them out." He knows us and calls us. When we feel unknown, rest in this truth. He knows your name. He is calling you. You matter to Him.

"Lord, I will listen for Your call."

92

HE FEELS MERCY TOWARD US

There are so many scriptures that talk about the mercy of God. His mercy is always directed at His people, those who acknowledge Him as the One true God. There is no room for the worship of any other god or anything else. When we look at this while under duress, this rock-solid rule brings comfort we may not think about until we need its staunch, direct clarity. Let me explain.

Facing the scary diagnosis of sarcoma, an incredibly aggressive form of cancer, I found myself losing my faith. Sounds shallow of me, and yet there I was. The stats on survival were nonexistent. In fact, once diagnosed, one might live three years. Maybe less. I saw my future and my faith reeling in a sea of dark, murky waters. It felt like everything around me was fading, my hope and faith in God and His ability included. Who can stand against Sarcoma? Who could provide support, direct our steps, or soothe our terrified souls? Then one day, while reading Deuteronomy, I saw it. God's absolute resolve in who He is. His unmistakable identity as the One True God of all things. And I saw His complete mercy in this proclamation.

"For the Lord your God is a merciful God. He will not leave you or destroy you or forget his covenant with your fathers that he swore to them" (Deuteronomy 4:31). This verse rests at the end of a section of scripture starting in verse 15, where God unmistakably insists on no worship of anything else. No other gods. Period. He is adamant about it. He leaves zero room for any other reliance on any other thing for His people. Why? Because He will not share His glory with anything or anyone else. But why is that?

I had it explained to me once in this way. Imagine you're drowning. Your ship has gone down in the pitch black of night. You see nothing. You only feel the icy cold water engulfing you and have nothing to hold on to. But God is headed towards you. He has the boat, lots of room, and the strength to rescue you completely. Would He tolerate another voice drawing you away from His saving? Knowing no one else in the waters can save you? Would He allow distractions that waste what little energy you have left to fill you with false hope? Absolutely not! He loves you. He is the only one who can rescue you.

Now we can see His mercy in demanding that He alone be trusted and worshiped. He knows nothing else can save. He also knows there is nothing you will face that puts you out of His great grip of salvation. So, in this context, of God demanding His people not give their worship to or put their hope in anything else, He declares that He alone will show us mercy. His mercy. The kind of mercy that saves. When we have fallen into deep, dark, engulfing waters. He alone can save. And His heart is set on doing just that. Regardless of what you see or how you feel, even as the darkness closes in, Hold tight to this truth. And know God is merciful to us, and He alone can rescue us!

"Lord, Thank You that You are good to all." (Psalm 145:9)

93

HE FEELS
ABOUNDING IN LOVE

"The Lord is merciful and gracious…" (Psalm 103:8a) Mercy and grace. It's what Abba is. It's what He extends to us and pours over us. We may struggle to see this in hardship, but it is who He is. Always. "Slow to anger and abounding in steadfast love" (verse 8b). It is so true. Yet, when we are covered up in grief or loss, the truth of His character can fade under the weight.

I remember looking into the eyes of one of my daughters and seeing the bitter anger and disdain for a God who would let her dad die slowly before her eyes. How could God do this? Was He even a loving God? Her mind could not comprehend a God who would allow cancer to destroy her dad. She started to form her own view of God. And I realized so many of us do this. We go through horrible things. We see loved ones struggle. It does not make sense to us. So we immediately try to fit God into what we can understand. But our circumstances do not redefine God. Only God can tell us who He is. And He does. Plainly. In His word.

We serve a God whom we cannot comprehend, and that's a good thing. If we could figure Him out, would we need Him? What our hearts need in hardship is the working of His Holy Spirit, to tend to our brokenness and open our eyes to see hope in the darkness. Only God can do this. My daughter slowly began to respond to the prompting of the Holy Spirit. First, to come and spill all her anger and pain at His feet. She had raw, honest moments of questions and poured out her bitterness to Him. She started to notice that He didn't mind her anger. He stayed with her as she hurled her raw accusations and disappointments at Him. She also noticed no judgment from Him. No scolding or even correcting her. This softened her heart and opened her eyes and ears to see His truth and receive His comfort as she mourned her dad. She saw that God didn't give up on her. He was sticking with her through this process. By His Spirit, she found herself sticking with God. Her emotions moved from rage to sorrow, and the Great Comforter met her there and extended His love to her wounds. She eventually gave in to God's kindness in response to her harshness. She walks with Him to this day, even closer than before. That's what His abounding love does for us.

He is faithful when life hurts. He is generous with His love when we feel depleted. He shows us mercy and grace when we feel unworthy, abandoned, and forgotten. Bring Him your anger, confusion, accusations, and disappointments. He can handle them. He remains abounding in love for us. His heart is toward us. Let His Holy Word revive your mind when you feel heavy with grief. Take a moment and breathe in His presence. Count to five as you breathe in Jesus, and breathe out anything negative. When you do this, you slow down both your breathing and your thinking, and you are free to soak in His abounding love for you, his child.

"Abba, I rest in Your abounding love."

94

HE IS PATIENT WITH US

Patience is a virtue that is lost in hardship. Not at first. But for us, somewhere in the third year, we just grew impatient. Impatient with the care team. Impatient with the kids' crazy schedules and the fact that life decided to aggressively carry on despite our lack of sleep and lack of mental or physical energy. Impatient with each other as we were still learning how to help each other through this horrible mess of battling cancer together. Impatient. Frustrated. Wanting more from those around us, yet incapable of giving any more than we were giving ourselves.

Things got ugly with all the impatience floating around. And we had to pause, call out the problem, ask forgiveness a lot, and forgive as well. I know it was unearthly to even see how we were treating one another, much less be able to step away and let His Spirit change our impatient attitude. And that lesson really etched a truth about our Heavenly Father into my heart. It gave me a greater picture of His great love for His own.

God knows where we come from. He knows we are dust. Genesis 2:7 says, "Then the Lord God formed man out of dust from the ground and breathed into his nostrils the breath of life." He knows this about us because He is the One who formed us out of dust.

God is aware of our limitations, tendencies, and shortcomings. We grow impatient after some pressure is applied. Don't misunderstand. His knowing doesn't make excuses for us. He just knows who we are and what we're made of. He gets us. He knows what we start with and how we end up. Ecclesiastes 12:7 puts it this way: "...and the dust returns to the earth as it was, and the spirit returns to God who gave it." In this knowing, I stand in awe of our Creator God. He knows us, and yet He remains patient with us.

The Psalmist writes of God's patience towards us: "The Lord is compassionate and merciful, very patient, and full of faithful love" (Psalm 103:8). Here, we see David meditating on God's amazing love towards us and His patience with us. David knows a thing or two about getting impatient with people and circumstances and being impatient with himself as well. He knows he is imperfect and he appreciates that God is patient with him. When we're honest about ourselves, we can relate to David and his shortcomings. God deals with our imperfect souls with patience and mercy. Like David, we can rest assured in God's faithful love, even in our weaknesses.

In hardships, we grow impatient with ourselves, but God does not. He knows us. He loves us. He gives us His grace and new mercies every morning (Lamentations 3:22). When you feel impatient under the weight of your struggle, lift your eyes up and know He is patient with you.

"Lord, Thank You for Your patience."

95

HE SEES US AS HIS "FAVORED"

I remember sitting with one of my children as he faced a difficult milestone under the heartache of Dad being ill. He was going from middle school to high school and genuinely struggled to see where he fit into the overall scheme of life. We had to go deep into the Word of God to reset his identity. Rooted and anchored in Christ, regardless of the hardship we were walking through as a family.

If we're honest, as adults we need to remind ourselves that we, too, are rooted and anchored in Christ. Sometimes in hardship, we struggle to see where we fit in, especially when our circumstances don't make sense to us. We forget that God sees us as His favored children. And with His favor comes protection and all of His goodness. God, Creator of all living things, has an opinion of you. He has since before time began. We see in Genesis, through the story of Creation, how He separates us from the other living things He creates. We see how God made us in His likeness and put us in charge of the plants and animals.

Isaiah 43:4 shows us His special love for us: "Because you are precious in my eyes and honored, and I love you…" He sees us as His own special creation. And He pours out His favor on us because of His view of us. When we wrestle with things we don't understand, it's easy to forget how God sees us and what He thinks of us. He sees us as His sons and daughters, made in His image. Not because we are fully understanding of everything, or because everything is going well for us. Because He said so. We don't have the mind of God, and His thoughts and ways are higher than ours (Isaiah 55:9-10). We may not fully understand His thoughts but we can know what He has declared of us, His people.

Deuteronomy 7:6 clarifies for us, "For you are a people holy to the Lord your God. The Lord your God has chosen you to be a people for His treasured possession..." It's important to note that this declaration has no strings. He does not say unless we struggle or go through hardship. We already know our hardship serves a purpose, to fine-tune and grow us closer to perfection (James 1:4).

But we see more than this when we look further. He does not withhold from us. We can rest in this truth as we face the unknown. Let's allow our minds to be healed and reset with the word of our Lord, who has declared us a people holy to Himself. This is what we are rooted in. This is who God says we are. And he has put His favor on us for His glory.

Today, as you sit, facing the unknown. If you have forgotten who you are, and more importantly, Whose you are, let these scriptures bring you back to your Lord and Savior, and let His favor cover your weary mind and heart. He favors His own.

"Lord, cover me with Your favor as with a shield (Psalm 5:12)."

96

HE SEES US MADE NEW

What if you could have a new start? I vividly remember longing for a new start in the middle of our battle with cancer. The years of struggle we walked with Mark's bad health wore us out. We felt depleted and discouraged. We were tired, weary, and worn. Have you ever felt like what you've been through has taken the wind out of your sails? Ever needed a fresh start with fresh courage? Fresh energy? Fresh faith? There is good news! 2 Corinthians 5:17 carries a promise for those of us who are in Christ: "If anyone is in Christ, he is a new creation. The old has passed away; behold, the new has come." But this is not only true when we first accept Christ as our Savior. He continues to make us new.

He has reconciled us to Him, and now He is sanctifying us. He is the breath in our lungs, and therefore He revives us. Psalm 23:3 says He restores our soul. There are things in this world that wear us down. They rattle us. They steal our strength and can wither our hope. But we have Christ in us, renewing our minds and lifting our spirits as we sit quietly in His presence. He doesn't see the flaws and failures. He sees us as one of His sons or daughters, and therefore, being renewed daily. His work with us is ongoing. Philippians 1:6 says, "I am sure that He who began a good work for you will bring it to completion on the day of Jesus Christ." This is evidence that His good work is constant within. It revives, refreshes, and replaces our worn-out minds, bodies, and spirits with His truth. With His good works. With His plan to make us new in Him. We also have this hope that our struggle is renewing and strengthening us. "We know that the testing of our faith produces steadfastness" (James 1:2b). That's why, even as we are dragging our feet, drudging through our days at times, He tells us to "count it all joy when we meet trials of various kinds" (verse 2a).

He has a plan! He is making us new. Yes, with our trials. Yes, it is ongoing. Yes, today, as you read this with little strength. He sees you. He is working in your life with great gifts and draining sorrows you receive. He is making you new. It's a shift in thinking when we see that God Almighty has a good plan. He is refreshing us, growing us, breathing life into us, and using it all to carry out this renewing plan. When we feel weary, let's look to Him. Let us fix our eyes on Jesus. And rejoice in how He sees us, made new.

"Lord, revive me with Your Spirit."

97

HE DELIGHTS
IN OUR PRAISES

"The Lord takes pleasure in those who fear him, in those who hope in his steadfast love" (Psalm 147:11). Grief can cast a shadow over us. This makes it a challenge to praise Him. In fact, it can seem impossible to offer praise to God. Yet, it's in our grief that He sees the sacrifice of our praise. This brings Him delight. God welcomes our praises, whether they spring forth from hearts filled with joy or from hearts heavy with sorrow. During my time of grief, I must admit that my praise was sometimes obligatory. My heart ached while I attempted to offer praise to Abba Father. I struggled with what to be thankful for in that season of my life. Then God showed me that praise is focused on Him. His character. His faithfulness to carry out every promise. It's not centered on how I feel or what I am experiencing. God is good. He is Sovereign. He is the only one worthy of all praise. This helped me see my praise offering in a different light. I was not just going through the motions. I was not faking my praise. My God is the same yesterday, today, and tomorrow (Hebrews 13:8).

In times of grief, our praises also become a testimony to the transforming power of God's love. As I shift my thinking from my circumstances to a Holy God who has promised to make everything new and correct every wrong, I see the bigger picture of His purpose in my grief. This bigger picture transforms my thinking to focus on all of His promises. I begin to see Him using my grief to soften my heart, draw me into His presence, and use my circumstances to show others the goodness of God. And that brings such rich hope. It lifts my heart, and joy can rush in. Our praise draws us closer to the One who can restore our soul and carry us through the pain. Praising through our sorrow becomes an offering of trust and surrender. When we choose to lift our praise, we express our faith in His goodness, even amid our pain. Praising Him in our sorrow does not deny our pain, but it is a declaration that God is greater than our pain. Our praise ushers in His peace, which goes beyond our circumstances and our own understanding (Philippians 4:7). He takes the brokenness and makes us whole again as He delights in our praise. God's word says, "He inhabits the praise of His people" (Psalm 22:3). And we know that in His presence, we find solace from our suffering.

Though it may be hard to do, offering our praise in grief reshifts our thinking from sorrow to the Solution. It ushers us into His presence, where we find healing and hope. It reminds us that this world is temporary, and He has prepared our eternity. It feeds our minds and souls the spiritual nourishment we desperately need. And He delights in seeing us benefit through our praise. He also finds joy in the trust and surrender we are giving to our Good Father. Praise Him in the storm and watch your soul be satisfied in His delight.

"Lord, I praise You in the storm."

98

HE SEES US UNITED WITH HIM

I remember the day we were brave and ventured to Mexico for additional treatment for Mark. It was scary. We felt unsure and nervous. We knew we had done our research and much praying. Still, as we boarded the plane, it felt as if we had disconnected from everyone and everything we knew. Insurance was stopping at the border. Our trusted doctors of eight years would not greet us. Little did we know we would find an amazing staff with faith in our same God, much knowledge and insight, and wonderful doctors to love on us and help us heal.

It was such a great decision. Mark gained weight and energy and was refreshed. The doctors we met in Mexico became so encouraging to us after we better understood what Oasis offers their cancer patients. Yet, we felt so out of sorts in those first few hours. It felt like it was just me and Mark against the world. Ever felt that way in your hardship?

Difficult times cast a shroud of disjointedness and distance from what we know to be good, true, and helpful. We can feel as if we have stepped into an arena and are on our own. Nothing familiar. No helpful advice. No smiling faces. Just us and our hardship and a tough decision. But did you know? God does not see us as separate from Him. Not at any point in our hardship. Not in the scary times. Nor the dark, lonely times. Not in the times we mess up and make mistakes. He stays with us. In fact, He sees us as united with Him. Ephesians 2:13 tells us we have been brought near by the blood of Christ, "But now in Christ Jesus, you who were once far off have been brought near by the blood of Christ." It goes on to say, "For he himself is our peace" (vs. 14). Can you hear the security and faithfulness in these verses?

We are united with Christ through His blood, which never changes. His sacrifice is a done deal. Unable to be undone. When the darkest of times surrounds us. When we feel unsure, unsupported, or disjointed, we are united with Christ. Does this matter in our hardship? Absolutely. It changes everything. We have His source of strength. His very presence is our peace. His comfort through His Spirit. In Christ, we have all we need. Even in a foreign country, facing scary uncertainties. Always. Ever. We are one with Christ.

When your circumstances pull you away from comfort, familiarity, or support, know with certainty how God sees you. United. In those times remind yourself of this truth with a notecard in your purse or taped to your bathroom mirror. Look for ways to surround yourself with God's truth when you find yourself feeling unsure and distant from your Savior. I like to play Christ-focused music in the car or at home. Maybe even say out loud, or under your breath, the verse above, "Thank you, Lord, that I am brought near by Your blood today." He will agree with your spirit and it will remind you that He is near.

"Lord, unite me with You."

99

HE ENJOYS US!

It was a late, dark night. The kids, exhausted from driving back and forth to the hospital one hour away for the entire week, were glad to have the family under one roof again. Trying to catch up on some sleep, they all collapsed early that night. My husband, exhausted from a week-long hospital stay, passed out, happy to be in our bed. The whole house was quiet, yet I was restless. I could not get my brain to shut down. Then this verse entered my mind, "For the Lord takes pleasure in his people; he adorns the humble with salvation" (Psalm 149:4-5).

Have you considered this truth? He takes pleasure in us. Oftentimes, in hardship, we can forget this truth. We feel we are a burden with our constant needs. Our mind races to the urgency of our dire situation, and we panic-pray. Have you ever done that? I was reeling in our need, our lack, the pain my whole family was in. I headed to my prayer closet for some much-needed peace with Abba. But the more I "cast all my cares upon him, because he cares for me" (1 Peter 5:7), the more anxious I got. I started throwing pleas up, frantic, riddled with fear and worry. I call those panic prayers. You know, the ones where God isn't really present with you? You aren't really praying to Him, just going over all the problems and needs in your life. Panic. No faith required. I found myself not even thinking about God. Not sitting with Him. Just sitting in a closet alone, with all my anxious thoughts beating me over the head. I almost thought stopping my prayer and going to bed would be better. But then, I got a vision of God, calmly, quietly, smiling at me.

He didn't care that I was flailing my arms at him. He didn't care that I was not even listening. He enjoyed that I was present with Him. Once I let myself calm down and even smile sheepishly up at Him, He gushed in. He surrounded me with his great compassion, and I melted into a puddle. Suddenly, I was not even in my prayer closet. I was floating in His presence, consumed with the deep understanding and life-giving love of the One who made me. The one who enjoyed my company. The One who saw my heart, my need, my humanness. None of it pushed Him away. He waited for me to see Him. And before I could even apologize, He wrapped me up in His compassion for me, His child. He enjoys us coming to Him. Scripture tells us it is impossible to please God without faith. Have you ever allowed yourself to realize that with our faith, we please Him? And how much faith? The size of a mustard seed will do. He does the rest.

When you find yourself panic-praying, stop. Smile and know that God is right there with you, with compassion that changes our hearts, minds, countenance, and hope. Receive His compassion today.

"Abba, I receive. Thank You for loving me."

100

HE FEELS COMPASSION TOWARDS US

In the heavy battle of cancer, my husband was struggling with nausea and struggling for his life. Trying to maintain normalcy for our kids, we had our athletes in their sports as usual. One of our daughter's basketball coaches was such a generous man. He went out of his way to pick her up and drop her off after each practice when I couldn't leave Mark's side. Once a week, as he dropped her off, he brought a huge feast for the family. He gushed compassion on us. I once asked him why, and his response was so genuine. He said, "That's what you do, Tina. You help where you can." And he did. The entire season that man lavished us with compassion. He never made our daughter feel she was a burden. And he was always there willingly, providing a good meal for us on top of all his kindness. He had compassion for us. He lavished us with his time and met specific needs with a willingness that seemed to have no end.

God treats us with this same compassion. In fact, even better. In our struggles, we forget that as His children, He has already met our greatest need. Our souls are secure in Him. He has sent His son to die and pay the price for our sins to be erased. He made a way for our sins to be covered. He takes away the punishment of sin, which is death. The Psalmist said it this way, "Yet he, being compassionate, atoned for their iniquity and did not destroy them..." (Psalm 78:38). Our daughter's coach was kind and showed us compassion, but God's love meets deeper needs than anyone else ever could. In our hardship, let's remember that as we stand now, in the throes of our grief and struggle, Abba has lavished us with compassion in the forgiveness of our sins. And we have this hope as well, in Lamentations, "The steadfast love of the Lord never ceases; his mercies never come to an end; they are new every morning; great is your faithfulness" (Lamentations 3:22-23).

This means no matter what we face here on earth, we are covered. God invites us, again and again, to come to Him: "...Return to the Lord your God who is gracious and merciful, slow to anger and abounding in steadfast love..." Joel 2:13. This invitation has no limits. Is there anyone else who shows such compassion to us? "Who is a God like you, pardoning iniquity and passing over transgression..." Micah 7:18. When you feel overwhelmed and forgotten in your struggle, rest your head on the shoulders of His great, never-ending compassion, and receive His care for you, just as you are.

"Lord, Your compassions are never ending."

ACKNOWLEDGEMENTS:

"What do I do now?" I asked my husband. His time on this earth as my husband, leader, teammate, and friend was coming to an end. We both knew it. As we sat holding each other, Mark was quiet for a moment. Then simply said, "Write, Tina."

Early on we both learned that writing was a gift God had given me. By that, I mean a gift that brought healing to my weary, sometimes terrified, soul. Abba Father created me to write it all out, my fears, worries, heartaches, and frustrations, sure. But also my Ever-Present Help in every situation that would ever come into my life.

Mark getting cancer at 41 years old threw us both for a loop. Our kids too. In the darkest moments of this journey with this aggressive cancer, it was God who first whispered into my soul, "Write, Tina. Float beside me. Observe all I am doing, and share what you learn with whomever will listen."

It started as a vehicle to inform Mark's clients, and our friends and family of updates regarding Mark's treatments, victories, and prayer requests, as we battled cancer. After Mark's death, it continued to be an outlet of Abba Father's goodness to me in my deepest need.

This book is a result of the profound encouragement of both my loving, edifying husband and my Lord and Savior. The One who gave me such a perfect partner, the One who put inside of me a desire to write and share all He has shown me throughout my whole life. The One who led me to Hope*books and Brian Dixon, the talented and generous leader/instructor/encourager, and Abby McDonald, my editor. She has tirelessly answered every question and concern, and has taken the simple words I write, polished them up, and made them worthy of our King and Savior. I am so grateful for her professional and compassionate input on each page of this book.

In addition, I have to thank each person who took the time to reach out and encourage me to write. There are too many of you to name, but please know that each one of you is held close to my heart. Writing this book has been such a vulnerable and exposed experience. I have cried over every page, begging the Holy Spirit to seep into each word, that it would meet someone in the middle of their darkest moments, and pour out His healing, perfect love. I have been carried on the wings of every word of encouragement, every prayer offered on my behalf, and every one of you who willingly gifted me with hope through this process. To say I am grateful is such an understatement. You know who you are, and my deepest gratitude is extended to you.

Finally, this book is propped up by the unending encouragement of my children, and their spouses, a wealth of generosity Abba has lavished upon me. They continually believed in me when I struggled to stay focused, to stay vulnerable, and to believe that this book was Abba's next thing for me. William, Alli, Emma Lynn, Micah, Kathryn, Josiah, and Sidney…you are my treasures and I am honored to be in your lives. I love you.

All praise and glory is to my Lord, my Savior, my King, my Friend, Jesus Christ.

MEET THE AUTHOR

Tina, a devoted mother of four exceptional children and a widow, spent 25 ½ years in a deeply cherished marriage to a man whose love for God and family knew no bounds. Their journey together, marked by love, loss, and unwavering faith, serves as a testament to the goodness and faithfulness of God.

In every chapter of her life, Tina has witnessed the hand of an Involved, Loving, Present God who lavishes His blessings upon His children, even in the midst of trials. Through her words, she invites readers to experience the grace and presence of our Heavenly Father, regardless of the circumstances they may be facing.

Tina's hope is that as you journey through her story, your faith will be strengthened, your resolve to live out your faith deepened, and your heart uplifted by the boundless love of Abba Father. May you join her in celebrating and absorbing His grace together, finding strength and courage for whatever path lies ahead.

www.ingramcontent.com/pod-product-compliance
Lightning Source LLC
Chambersburg PA
CBHW020234130626
46549CB00005B/1890